Living the Way

Quaker spirituality and community

Ursula Jane O'Shea

THE TWENTY-EIGHTH
JAMES BACKHOUSE LECTURE ✪ 1993

First published in 1993 © by Australia Yearly Meeting
as the 28th James Backhouse Lecture.
This edition © Quaker Books, 2003
Friends House, 173 Euston Road, London NW1 2BJ

http://www.quaker.org.uk

We acknowledge with thanks the use, on our covers,
of a detail from *Gracechurch Street Meeting, London,
circa 1770* by an anonymous artist, from the Library of
Friends House, London.

ISBN 0 85245 348 5

Designed by Jonathan Sargent
Cover design scheme: Peter Daniels
Printed by Thanet Press Ltd
Text typeface: Charter ITC, 10.5 on 14 pt

Contents

The James Backhouse Lectures

This is one of a series of lectures instituted by Australia Yearly Meeting of the Religious Society of Friends on the occasion of the establishment of that Yearly Meeting in 1964.

This lecture was delivered in Brisbane on 2 January 1993 during the Yearly Meeting.

James Backhouse was an English Friend who visited Australia from 1832 to 1838. He and his companion, George Washington Walker, travelled widely but spent most of their time in Tasmania. It was through their visit that Quaker Meetings were first established in Australia.

From the beginnings of Quakerism in the seventeenth century, Friends developed a tradition of 'travelling under concern', being guided by God to visit places near and far to experience the conditions of people there and to minister to them as the Spirit led. James Backhouse and George Washington Walker drew added inspiration from nineteenth-century evangelicalism as they sought to share spiritual refreshment and humanitarian concerns with settlers and colonial authorities.

Australian Friends hope that this series of lectures will bring fresh insights into truth, often with reference to the needs and aspirations of Australian Quakerism.

About the author

Janey O'Shea grew up in northern Australia. As a young woman she followed the path of Franciscan spirituality as a member of a religious community. She has worked in a variety of capacities: as a teacher, a lecturer, a prison officer and a pastoral care worker in a major Brisbane hospital. She met Friends while studying at the University of Lancaster in 1981, joining Queensland Regional Meeting after she returned to Brisbane. There she has served as a Regional Meeting elder, as a member of Australia Yearly Meeting's Quaker Race Relations Committee, and as Convener of Friends' Book Supplies Committee during the establishment in Brisbane of the Margaret Fell Bookshop. In 1987 Janey first attended Woodbrooke College as a student, returning in 1990 as Friend-in-Residence and Australia Yearly Meeting representative at the First International Theological Conference for Quaker Women. In 1992 she accepted appointment as Quaker Studies Tutor at Woodbrooke for three years. On her return to Australia she took up a post in adult faith education in the Catholic diocese of Rockhampton. In this work she travels regularly to small communities throughout central Queensland.

The name 'London Yearly Meeting' was changed to
'Britain Yearly Meeting' from 1995.

Introduction

Modern Friends of the unprogrammed tradition are often reluctant to generalise about our collective Quaker experience, at least without qualifications or the familiar disclaimer, 'I can't speak for all Friends'.

Lack of dogmatism in matters of faith and of the Spirit is one of our great strengths as a community. It is probably the first quality which attracted many of us who joined the Society as convinced Friends. This character trait of modern Quakerism has its roots in the experience of early Friends, who found that real spirituality came from the inward guide, not from any outward authority, even scripture. Driven by the force of their inward experience, these Friends sought to make the same personal encounter with God available to everyone. If their experience lacked dogmatism, it did not lack certainty.

This is a distinction modern Friends can fail to make. Rejecting dogmatism which relies on outward authorities to prove its authenticity or to exercise power, we have also lost the confidence to testify to our spiritual experience and share it gladly.

This loss has increasingly individualised our experience of Quakerism. We are a diverse group of people, who are more often aware of our differences than of our common experience as Friends.

In this lecture I want to affirm that when Friends comply with the searching demands of the inward Light, we will find sure and certain guidance directing our lives, individually and corporately. Living under this guidance, members of the Religious Society of Friends have three fundamental life choices in common: we have chosen a spirituality, in a faith community, lived according to a Quaker Way. We may articulate these choices differently, but they underpin our unity and identity.

Spirituality. We have chosen a spiritual dimension to our lives which directs us from within. This choice we have in common with people from all religious traditions, and outside them, who look beyond material reality for a meaningful life.

Community. We have committed ourselves to participate in a community where we can express our spirituality and strengthen one another to meet its challenges. This choice we have in common with women and men who understand human beings not only as individual entities but also as a corporate body in relationship with the universe and with the divine, however it is conceived.

The Quaker Way. We have been born to, or adopted, a Quaker inheritance which can help us interpret our inward experiences, maintain a corporate spiritual life sustaining one another, and act together to transform our world. This choice we have in common with others who live by a habit of divine guidance in personal and community life, in the tradition of George Fox, Margaret Fell and early Friends.

To explore these choices I will begin by introducing the experience and meaning of spirituality in our contemporary context. There are limitations and important potential in exploring spirituality at the close of the twentieth century. These background influences are shaping Quakerism, and every religious tradition in the affluent world.

The substance of this lecture moves from spirituality in general to address the particular Quaker experience of spirituality, the Quaker Way. It is not fashionable to seem self-absorbed with the particularities of one's own religious tradition. It risks being elitist, appearing to devalue what other religious traditions have to offer spiritual seekers. Although grateful for what we learn from other traditions, we need to ask why the unique Quaker spiritual path is not more familiar to us nor more widely taught to members and newcomers, and to probe the impact of decreasing familiarity with Quaker spirituality on the transmission of an ongoing Quaker Way.

As I have prayed and tapped this lecture into existence on my Mac a difficult and violent gospel parable has slowly crept into the foreground: *The Parable of the Talents*. This story has grown to symbolise the spiritual treasures I want to speak about in this lecture: personal treasures and community treasures.

The Parable of the Talents is about a cautious, timid soul (a lot like me, I've come to think) who tries to get by, playing it safe, hoping to stay out of the dark of his master's disfavour. He has a small treasure which he tries to protect from all risk. In the story, his timidity is punished and his very caution earns him expulsion from the light.

Jesus' parable reflects on the responsibilities of those entrusted with divine gifts. Such gifts are not private treasures; we must use them, even take some risks with them. We cannot bury them to keep them safe from our own inadequacy. In being too careful, the third servant in the parable devalued the importance of the treasure which had been entrusted to him. The ruler instructed:

> So take the talent from him, and give it to him who has the ten talents. For to every one who has will more be given, and he will have abundance; but from him who has not, even what he has will be taken away. (Matthew 25:28–29)

The ruler's words were harsh, and the sentence which followed a cruel one.

In the course of being pursued by this parable I began to wonder: what if the ruler was not administering punishment for the servant's behaviour, but describing the inevitable consequences of what he had done? What if the spiritual gifts we have received are not static treasures? Perhaps we are to use them or lose them.

Without use, even small, well-hoarded spiritual treasures may leave us dry. Spiritual experience and gifts are enlivening, functional and transformative only when their impact flows over into the daily life of the person and a wider community.

If this is true for each of us as individuals, it is also true for us as a Quaker community. We have been entrusted with a spiritual Way of which we are but the temporary custodians. A gift to us, we pass the Quaker Way on to others, transformed and augmented by our experience. In the image of the parable, transmitting our religious tradition to new Friends is not only returning the capital of the original investment, it has our interest added too.

The vital essence of a religious tradition or spiritual Way, passed from one generation to the next, is known as its 'charism'. 'Charism' means a divine gift or talent. Like the servants of the parable, we have been entrusted with such a gift in the Quaker Way.

1

Spirituality

A T-shirt passed me in the street, with a well-dressed young man inside. I read it coming and going:

LIFE'S A BITCH . . . AND THEN WE DIE

Meeting the unavoidable pain of life with lean hope, and despairing that there is anything more, is a common human experience, but the T-shirted young man jolted me because of the relish or defiance with which he announced his despair.

Our search for meaning in life commonly see-saws. When the daily round is sufficiently satisfying or distracting, big 'why' questions about the meaning of human life seem less important. When everyday life is uneasy, painful or destructive, urgent questions about the ultimate purpose of life are likely to break through. But not always. At times, we ease the pain of everyday realities by reorganising the components – more work, a new lover, a career change – or by distractions. As a popular car sticker says, 'When the going gets tough, the tough go shopping'.

If our efforts to occupy or distract ourselves fail, and unease persists, we may begin to look for another kind of meaning in our life. The search for meaning within, and beyond, everyday realities can trip us over into the territory of our lives I call spirituality. This territory can be unfamiliar, even for those who already consider themselves religious. In fact, it may be more difficult for those who are self-assured in their religion to fall into the stark new land of spirituality. John Wilhelm Rowntree, a 'birthright Friend' born into a Quaker family, was diagnosed as having a terminal illness in his mid-twenties. He expressed his discovery of the difference between spirituality and religiosity in the evangelical terms of Friends of his day:

> I am, shall we say, the average man... If anyone were to charge
> me with unorthodoxy I should be painfully shocked. I read the
> Bible, perhaps sometimes wondering what I have read five

minutes afterwards. I go certainly once, perhaps under favourable circumstances, twice, to church, chapel or meeting. I don't understand what is meant by the Trinity or the atonement... Christ, I say, is my Saviour, by which I mean (if I were ever so brutally frank with myself, which I am not) that he will leave me alone in this world, and save me in the next. So I go on. Now and then someone upon whose companionship I depend is called beyond the grave. On such occasions I am deeply touched... And then the tide of life, business and pleasure flows in again. The gap is filled. I forget and once more am satisfied to live on the surface... But let us suppose that the strong blow of some great catastrophe were to smite me. Something that destroyed the routine of self-pleasing and compelled me to face the realities which I have so steadfastly shirked. Let it be some permanent physical restriction like blindness, or some financial disaster... Where do I stand now?... Everything is bitter, life and the interminable future are desolate. Suddenly I realise that my Christ was a lay figure. I made him and draped him myself. I realise that at the heart of what I called my religion was but selfishness... and that my insincerity has brought upon me the doom of spiritual emptiness...[1]

Spirituality as meaning-maker

Spirituality is a meaning-maker which answers ultimate ('and then we die') questions, but also answers questions about the ('life's a bitch') grind of the daily round. An adequate spirituality must address both these dimensions. Quaker philosopher John Macmurray expressed it this way:

> A spirituality that does not seek and secure its material embodiment is imaginary and unreal. A material life that is not spiritually directed is a meaningless quest for power and more power for its own sake.[2]

The first difficulty in exploring spirituality is to take both its mystery and its pragmatisms seriously. We need to accept that at the heart of spirituality is a transcendent experience: something or someone – more than we can point to, more than we have words for

– touches our lives, suffusing us with meaning beyond the satisfactions of the material world. At the same time, we accept that spirituality, as experienced by bodily beings, is immanent: grounded in the world, a potential guide for our actions, our words, our life. We need to hold the tension of spirituality as both immanent and transcendent; here but not here; now but not yet.

The second difficulty arises out of the great variety of forms of spirituality and the growing connections between them in the modern world. In a multitude of ways human beings have experienced the transcendent and interpreted its significance for human life; and all cultures have proposed answers about the present and ultimate meaning of the human condition. In our shrinking world the varieties of religious experience can no longer be regarded as isolated or distinct traditions. Indigenous cultures have transposed elements from surrounding dominant cultures into their religious life, and a 'notable upsurge in the quest for varying forms of religious experience' in the west has also affected mainstream religions. In the context of the Catholic church, Graham Dann noted:

> There has been a steady increase in mysticism patterned on oriental religions, where Yoga is largely advocated by the Benedictines, while Zen Buddhism is mostly the prerogative of the Jesuits and Carmelites.[3]

The third difficulty is that over the last 150 years western culture has squeezed spirituality into a pretty strange box: making it intellectually accessible yet experientially unfamiliar. In this age of information technology it is easier to review the world's literature on human spirituality than it is to find an experienced guide for one's own spiritual search. Growing up in a culture inexperienced in spirituality, and reticent about it too, leaves many people with no anchor point when life gets empty or purposeless. In our culture the most convenient tools to treat spiritual malaise are psychological ones. Although often helpful, these are unable to take us beyond the purely human experience to the place where another mysterious reality touches the human heart.

The fourth difficulty is that there is no such thing as 'raw' experience. Spiritual experience can only have an impact upon someone if they can interpret and make sense of it within the already existing framework of their thought and life.

> There is no such thing as 'spirituality in general'. Every spiritual search is and must be guided by a particular literature, practice and community of faith.[4]

In my own inner journey I have found a reciprocal relationship between the religious traditions which have formed me and shaped how I perceive and interpret my experience; and my experience which will, over time, become a part of the tradition itself.

As detached observers we could examine the phenomena of spirituality from many angles. However, as travellers who want answers to personal questions we cannot explore spirituality from all its possible directions at once. My approach is that of a traveller, not an observer. My guides will be the traditions of Friends past, the practice of Friends present and whatever I can say of my own experience of the journey thus far. I will talk about some of the particular challenges to spirituality which I see for the Religious Society of Friends in our time.

To begin I sketch briefly the status of spirituality, as transcendence and as immanence, in western culture. We live out the Quaker Way in a culture which shapes the possibilities and the challenges of our spiritual journey. In the main body of the lecture I examine our inherited Quaker riches and consider personal and corporate spirituality in the present-day life of our Meetings. I close by pointing to some issues to be addressed by the Society of Friends to move forward in a spiritually enriching way.

This adventure into spirituality will track the two clues given us by the prophetic T-shirt: spirituality as meaning-maker for the here and now, and spirituality as the transcendent meaning-maker which takes us beyond ourselves and sustains us even if all else fails.

'And then we die' spirituality: a search for transcendence

> Where there is no vision, the people perish. (Proverbs 29:18)

In the 'Narnia' books by C.S. Lewis, most adventures begin with a wonderful piece of furniture. On the outside it is a large wardrobe. Through the door, behind the clothes, is a different and mysterious reality where there are tests to pass, evil to overcome, people to meet, good to do and ships to sail.

Most mainstream social and scientific maps of western culture show only the outside of the wardrobe, that is, everyday reality where fixed 'laws' rule the universe, and what is real can be measured. The world behind the wardrobe does not appear on these cultural maps. They generally dismiss spiritual experiences as, at best, a little quirky, despite consistent evidence from history and anthropology that human beings of diverse cultures commonly experience 'other worlds', or this world behaving in a 'non-lawful' way. Theologian/anthropologist Karl Rahner suggested that all human beings have the capacity for the core mystical experience of 'being orientated to God'. He sees this capacity, like the Quaker understanding of the Light Within everyone, as an essential element of human life which can be repressed but not destroyed.[5]

As the dominant religious tradition of the west, Christianity has tried to regulate which kinds of religious or spiritual experiences were lawful, and which were not. From the early days of the church, patriarchy dominated Christian theology and history and supported a hierarchical order of creation, redemption and spirituality. The authority of man over woman and clergy over laity have been essential to patriarchal Christianity's view of the created order.[6]

However, a fragile but resilient counter-strand of the Christian story has supported the individual's direct access to ultimate Truth by inward inspiration. Direct intuitive knowledge of the divine has been highly valued in parts of the tradition although usually viewed with suspicion, and often repressed, by guardians of orthodoxy. Quakerism has its roots in this alternative strand of the Christian tradition, which has nurtured many others from canonised Franciscans to heretical Beguines.

The traditional Christian term for the kinds of experiences which intimately linked the believer and divine was 'ecstasy': its Greek root meant 'to put out of place'. This neatly captured the essence of a transcendent experience which dislocated everyday reality and interrupted ordinary human awareness with something out of place, 'utterly other'.

In our culture of material plenty, transcendent or mystical experiences seem so out of place they are usually kept private. But there is now evidence all around us that many people are looking for meanings or experiences deeper than those provided by everyday reality. Growing churches like the Pentecostal ones are marked by their community endorsement and support for ecstatic spiritual experiences. Other alternatives are found in the smorgasbord of 'spiritual opportunities' on offer in any large city. Usually popularised for easy consumption, sometimes marketed for profit, the spiritual experiences vary widely: a course in Sufi dancing, a retreat on Christian mysticism, or a fire walk at the end of a weekend course.

Surprisingly, a significant number of people who are looking for fresh religious experience are already involved in a church and want to supplement the spiritual diet available to them. It would be a mistake to assume that those looking further than their regular church are less committed religiously. The search for personal religious experience is indicative of a greater spiritual need, a need not satisfied by institutional religious experience. As in George Fox's time, many people today feel that contemporary Christian institutions have lost their fundamental reason for existence: their ability to facilitate human experience of the immanent/transcendent God. The plethora of alternative spiritual experiences on offer suggests that many in our culture find a significant gap in their lives.

George Fox understood the human longing to lead a meaningful life. He had lived with the pain of that longing in his own life for years and grew disillusioned with the spiritual pretences that people put up. He was especially harsh with two kinds of pretence: those whose pious poses were not enlivened by *feeling* the power of God; and those 'Ranters' who sought the transports of spiritual experience without translating them into an upright life and the demands of Christian fellowship. In these attitudes, we see George Fox's recognition of the two dimensions of spirituality: its transcendence and its immanence.

For us, too, the wellspring of spirituality is its transcendent dimension: the experience which puts us out of our place into God's space where we find a new way (God's Way) to live: in our time, and outside our time. But the validation of spirituality lies in its immanent dimension as we strive to live it in our daily life, letting it spiral out to enrich a faith community which has nurtured us and our spiritual experiences.

Let us now turn from the transcendent experience itself to the experience in context, in the life of individuals and in the life of their community.

'Life's a bitch' spirituality: transforming daily life

> What does the Lord ask of you? To act justly, love tenderly and walk humbly with your God. (Micah 6:8)

A significant obstacle to bringing spiritual experience into the daily round is the inadequacy of language to express the ineffable. Lack of language can suppress a religious experience completely. A limited 'vocabulary' for spirituality can restrict its growth or its capacity to reach all aspects of daily life.[7]

We shape our experience by using the language we have at hand to express it. But any language we use will already have been shaped by experiences within a religious tradition or culture. It is difficult to find language to express religious experience because increasing secularisation has eroded familiarity with, and the usefulness of, theological language.[8] For many of us that language has become a barrier to religious experience.

In writing this lecture I have struggled with the tension between speaking of the Quaker tradition using historical terms of reference, including much 'God-language', and the need to find authentic contemporary language for the ongoing Quaker Way. I have been encouraged by the example of early Friends who, faced with a language that was no longer capable of containing their new faith experience, were nonetheless able to adapt that language to dismantle the outmoded structures.

Powerful experiences of the divine call us to do two things: to cross the bounds of everyday reality to experience the divine ('crossing over'), and to integrate what we find 'over there' into our life here and now ('living a spiritual Way').

Crossing over. Being on a spiritual path means, first, confronting our motives. Intimate experiences with the divine, if we seek only self-enhancement or spiritual status, will impoverish rather than transform us or our daily life.

Next, we must face the fact that the inward search brings pain and disruption as well as joy and simplicity.

> Throughout the history of civilisation the great traditions have offered human beings a door on the other side of which there stretches the long and difficult path to self knowledge... In the past the door has been well guarded by the institutions and forms of tradition. What does it mean, then, that these guardians seem to have vanished in the present age?[9]

Religious traditions committed to mystical experience do not teach the content of the experience; they selectively pass on to individuals the community's knowledge about how to manage it. A religious group cannot pass on the mystical experience, but it can teach new members access modes and control techniques as a way of transmitting the group's experience and sustaining a unified tradition.

Living a spiritual Way. Our spiritual experiences confront our everyday reality, but the two are not interchangeable. They need to be integrated into a balanced life to avoid the perils of fanaticism, emotionalism and other forms of religious extremism.

Integrating transcendent experience into ordinary life is a lifelong task. For most of us such experiences are rare, or occur in clusters, and our lives need time to catch up. Unexpected encounters with the divine are apt to take some getting used to. We have to accept the authenticity of the experience, despite its otherness; and then let go as it unsettles our complacency and rearranges our lives. New understandings from a transcendent experience can overthrow familiar categories, disrupting our sense of control. When empowering spiritual experiences invade our lives, the support of a community is crucial, providing a company of like-minded souls with whom to rejoice and to benefit from the fruits of the experience.

Communal imagery, theology and expectations will shape the spiritual experiences of the individuals in that community. Put negatively, the communality limits the experience of its members, pressuring them to conform to accepted group norms. Put positively, the communality makes spiritual experience accessible to the individual, and able to be shared, by offering an intelligible, if inadequate, framework of interpretation.

Religious experience and the Quaker Way

The Quaker Way has always looked to both the immanent and transcendent dimensions of spirituality. It holds that life's 'and then we die' questions are already answered within each of us, if only we'll listen; and that attending to the divine guidance within will transform and empower us when 'life's a bitch'.

Living out the immanent and transcendent aspects of spirituality as a Friend has never been a private matter. Quaker structures depend on the shared inward experiences of members as the basis for worship, the ordering of business, and social and humanitarian action. The Quaker Way takes on faith the seemingly irrational proposition that the inspirations of individuals can lead a community to unity and spiritual power, not to chaos and dismemberment.

Trusting inward experience was the founding impetus of the Quaker Way. As Quakerism became more organised, transcendent experience retained two roles in the community: a prophetic role through which the religious experiences of an individual may challenge and transform the community; and a conserving role through which the religious experience of the community enables it to protect itself from extremes of religious enthusiasm.

Spiritual power begins with individuals. The power of the inward experience is theirs, and theirs is the responsibility to examine their motives and to use the fruits of the experience in daily life. As William Braithwaite pointed out in the Third Swarthmore Lecture in 1909, '... it is with individuals rather than communities that new truth originates'.[10]

Individual experience can be enriched, intensified and augmented in the setting of the spiritual community. Balanced by corporate discernment, it can completely transform that community. The life and concerns of John Woolman are a classic example of this reciprocal process.[11] A spiritual community strengthens and steadies its members, nurturing them as they gain experience, and passing on a communal wisdom which a lifetime of individual searching may never uncover.

The nurturing and conserving roles of a community can anchor us when our spiritual resources fluctuate, drying up or overflowing. In return, individual transcendent experiences forge prophetic voices to inspire, energise and transform the community in which they live.

After three hundred years we may be justified in taking an optimistic view of the achievements and resilience of the Quaker Way, and the success with which it has lived out its prophetic and conserving roles. However, to live the Quaker Way faithfully in our own time and land is not to try to repeat what early Friends were called to do, or to cling to whatever Quaker forms we have inherited in this Yearly Meeting. What we share with Friends who have gone before us is a task and some fine tools. Our task is to inaugurate the Way of God in this time and in this land; our tools are our personal experience of the Light Within, and our corporate experience in using collective guidance to discover and enact God's will in the world. To do this we must not become more like early Friends, but more like ourselves as we are in the eye of God.

Religious organisations exist to promote and to control religious experience. These complementary but contradictory goals create an inherent tension in all kinds of religious groups, from established churches to informal prayer meetings, from monasteries to charismatic congregations. How a group balances control of religious experience with the promotion of that experience will shape both its spirituality and its structures. That is to say, the form of organisation is derived from the way the group reconciles the prophetic power of transcendent experiences with its corporate need to survive.

Religious traditions have solved this dilemma in different ways. Early Friends rejected the solutions they saw in Catholicism and Puritanism. The Roman Catholic church gave the authority to discern the truth of individual inspiration to a hierarchy committed primarily to the service of the organisation. Puritans put no intermediaries, other than scripture itself, between 'man' and God, but regulated the anarchic potential of their belief by emphasising the authority of the (male) householder in the domestic sphere, and the rule of the 'saints' over the ungodly in public life.

The unique Quaker balance of personal spiritual experience and corporate authority goes back to the foundation of Quakerism, to the lifetime of George Fox and early Friends. The evolution of Quakerism in various parts of the world has been marked by great diversity, but it has consistently accorded authority to inward spiritual experience. The thread of personal inspiration kept Quakerism alive across three centuries, and a counter-thread of corporate discipline kept it safe amid the vagaries of time and culture.

Quakerism viewed as a religious community

In the chapters that follow, I will outline the development of the spirituality of the Religious Society of Friends, so that we may better understand the raw materials, the potential and the limitations of the heritage we have to work with in living a Quaker Way at the end of the twentieth century. This discussion is structured around a sociological model of the life cycle of religious communities. It assumes that it is more useful to discuss Quakerism as a religious community than as an hierarchically established church.

A religious organisation is not static, because its prophetic, preserving and nurturing functions are in constant motion: shaped by interpretations of the past, the contemporary culture, and the personalities and capacities of those who are currently living in the tradition. Most sociological debate about the nature of religious organisations has not been inclusive of the Quaker experience. The peculiarities of Quakerism do not fit easily in the contested sociological categories of sect, denomination or church. The most helpful model I have found for considering Quakerism is one developed by sociologists Raymond Fitz and Lawrence Cada.[12] Their model was originally used to interpret the rapid devolution of religious orders after Vatican II. Comparisons of Quakerism to religious orders have been made elsewhere[13], but I find five major ways in which the growth and development of the Quaker Way relates closely to the pattern of a religious order.

First, both Quakerism and the mystical traditions of religious orders presumed that God's revelation was ongoing among God's faithful people, and that human beings had the capacity to share in the experience of divine disclosure.

Second, both Quakerism and religious orders considered a serious spiritual life not an option but a requirement. Religious men and women undertook a 'Life of Perfection' by their vows, and were helped to live it with the support of their community. The Quaker tradition has always taken Jesus' command to be perfect as a serious proposition for a Friend, and at most times in our history members of our community have been keen to help each Friend get on with it!

Third is the voluntary nature of the commitment, both to membership and to following the religious community's traditions and norms. Like religious communities, Quakerism faces the task of passing on a tradition to newcomers who are attracted to some aspect of its life, but who on arrival may know little about the actual tradition. What is passed on must be more than mere knowledge of the tradition: newcomers must be drawn into actively living the shared spiritual Way.

Fourth, Quakerism and religious orders are currently in a period of transition. In the past both kinds of communities had isolated themselves from the influences of the outside world. Religious orders usually isolated themselves physically. Friends' isolation was ensured by their closed social network and particularities of dress and speech.[14] In modern times, closed religious groups have experienced similar problems as they became more open, undergoing a process of transformation and determining which parts of the tradition were to be reclaimed and renewed, and which were to be discarded.

Finally, Friends diverge from other churches in the way we have structured the challenging, preserving and nurturing tasks of a spiritual community. The majority of Christian churches entrust these functions to a person specially trained and formally installed in this role by a community. A Friends' meeting, like a religious community, believes it will find the necessary gifts within each group, not because of the chance occurrence of human talents among its members, but because the Spirit will call and empower individuals to serve as they are needed.

Raymond Fitz and Lawrence Cada proposed that the life cycle of a religious community followed five phases of growth and decline: foundation, expansion, stabilisation and breakdown, succeeded by a period of transition during which the community could die out, survive at a minimal level or enter into a new phase of growth. In chapters 2, 3 and 4, I show how the present-day Quaker balance of corporate and personal spirituality arose out of the merger of three elements of our early history: the spiritual experiences of George Fox and his charismatic teaching which founded the movement; the expansion of the movement across the world and its survival of persecution; and a stroke of organisational genius which stabilised Quaker life and transmitted Quaker spirituality to a new generation despite growing inertia and conservatism. In chapters 5 and 6 I examine contemporary forces of destabilisation and transition, and the prospects for renewal of the Quaker Way.

2

A generation of prophets: the foundation of Quakerism

New religious communities usually begin with an individual whose original or timely insights challenge and inspire others to a committed and renewed spiritual life. This initial period is marked by transcendent experiences; by a fresh and meaningful interpretation of the gospel and the role of Jesus in the lives of those who become involved; and by the attempt to live out the requirements of the gospel as a community. As more people respond to the Way opened to the founder, the group becomes larger and has to decide about how to organise itself, how to exercise authority, and how to relate to others outside the group. The development of Quakerism in seventeenth-century England was the story of one group who learnt to manage spirituality so that their founding charism remained powerful, ongoing and safe within a community context.

Life in mid-seventeenth century England was turbulent: the execution of a king, civil war, Commonwealth rule and a new king, all in a few short years. Two aspects of the period are remarkable: the extent to which common people participated in these momentous political events, and the serious religious interests which motivated their involvement.

Longing for meaningful religion was evident everywhere, but there was little agreement about solutions. There was a surfeit of answers to the ultimate questions of life and diverse suggestions as to how these answers could be applied in the daily life of church and state. Conservative Puritans wanted to supplant episcopacy (government by a bishop) with Presbyterianism (government by community elders) as the established church order. Others, of Anabaptist persuasion, preached the equality of God's election, arguing that working men should be ministers and preachers. Some radicals even allowed women to interpret the scriptures and to preach. Religious feelings overflowed into social and political action.[15] Some groups were millenarian, linking their agendas for political and social reform with an imminent Second Coming of Christ. The scope of the turmoil of the times may be judged by the complaint of conservatives that even the women who sold oysters from street carts 'locked their fish up, and trudged away to cry, "No bishop!"'.[16]

George Fox's spiritual experience

In the early 1640s George Fox shared the sense of religious longing of many around him. His life changed in 1647 when, in a series of transcendent experiences, he felt the vitality of Christ inside himself directing and comforting him, making him whole. Some of George Fox's experiences were visionary, others conveyed an inner awareness that something in himself and in the world had changed.

> Now was I come up in spirit through the flaming sword into the paradise of God. All things were new, and all creation gave another smell unto me than before, beyond what words can utter.[17]

In one of the most extraordinary insights of Christian mysticism, George Fox did not assume that his transcendent experiences were only a personal grace. He deduced that the experiences that he had had of divine guidance were available to everyone: Christ's presence and guidance were intimately accessible and active within each person, not as a precept of faith or dogma, but as their own experience. Furthermore, George Fox's great familiarity with scripture shaped a theological and social interpretation of inward experience which made sense to the people of his turbulent time. George Fox set out to address a message of hope to others who were desperately searching outside themselves for life's meaning.

In Puritan England, as in Catholic England before it, questions about salvation were living issues for ordinary people: how were you saved and how did you stay in this blessed state? Such religiously focussed anxiety is a long way from the experience of most modern Friends. It is hard for us to appreciate the comfort and originality of

George Fox's simple message for his contemporaries: salvation was at hand if you turned to the Christ Within you.

The experience of the Light Within

The power of George Fox's transcendent experiences and his tireless career of preaching and imprisonment led Evelyn Underhill to suggest that he was both a mystic and 'a "great active" of the first rank'.[18] George Fox did not try to draw people to himself as a teacher but directed them to the 'Light Within', to attend to their own inward guide, and obey it. His emphasis on the authority of one's inward guide came to characterise Quaker spirituality and facilitated the rapid expansion of the movement.

George Fox succeeded as a preacher by the obvious power and authenticity of his personal experience of the divine; and by his ability to relate these experiences to the scriptures, interpreting them afresh to address the most pressing issues for people of his day. Many early Friends were seeking 'real religion' at the time they heard George Fox preach. In Quaker terms they were not converted by his words but by the testimony of their own inward guide, who affirmed what they heard and led them to join the movement and transform their lives. His method of teaching was such that his followers did not become 'Foxites'; rather, he put them in touch with themselves and with each other.

Although each person's situation was unique, the same process of 'turning to the Light Within' was at the core of all Quaker spirituality. One of the attractions of the Quaker message was that access to these powerful experiences was not a complicated affair. It did not require the intervention of priest, ritual, ascetic practices, position or education; one had only to be 'open', 'still', and 'look within' to find the Light which would teach and lead.

Early Friends' experiences of the Light Within could be both joyous and terrifying. The Light searched them, showing them who they were and who they should/could be before God. They were 'convicted' and shown their sinfulness by the Light. Intense awareness of their sin and failure, and terror at the prospect of what the Light might demand of them, usually made these initial experiences extremely painful as well as enriching. The process of being searched by the Light was simply called 'the Cross'. Quaking was sometimes taken as a sign of the power of the inward experience with which a Friend wrestled.

It was only a beginning. Hearing and being convinced of the 'Truth', one then began a long process of learning to turn to the Light Within and to give over one's life to the authority of the inward guide. The Light showed up hidden sinfulness and self-deceptions, it led and guided and, most important, the Light empowered. For early Friends 'conversion' referred to the process by which a person, having been 'convicted' of their sin, began, under the power of the Christ Within, to convert their life to conformity with their inner guide.

Long silent meetings gave Friends space to face The Cross and to follow the Light. Opportunity for quiet reflection, and a supportive group among whom one could rest or be challenged, sustained new Friends as they integrated their transcendent experiences into the rest of their lives. When a new Friend chose to follow the demands of the Light it was usually a turning point. Most went on to live with extraordinary purpose and courage. The Light spoke clearly to them: the self was integrated and unified, willing to follow the inner guide at all times. Linked to the 'other' reality which guided and focussed their lives, early Friends did not keep tight boundaries between spiritual reality and ordinary life. Quaker journals indicated that powerful experiences were still likely to occur for Friends in times of extreme stress or persecution. Or if a Friend was reluctant to take up a particular 'leading' s/he would again be troubled by the searching power of the Light.

From the first days the Quaker experience of living by the Light was a call to community. The same Light which guided individual Friends was seen to guide the whole community, especially in worship. Corporate inspiration was the basis for a Quaker group's unity and made their style of worship possible. If the individual members of a meeting attended faithfully to the Light Within, their communal life would be ordered and unified. There were tragedies and compromises in the new Quaker movement as ways were sought to systematise the sense of unity Friends experienced when they submitted together to the Spirit's guidance.

The Light Within guided each person who attended to it faithfully, but it was also recognised that some Friends were particularly 'serviceable' in preaching the word of the Spirit. These were the prophetic voices of the first generation of Friends. Many of them travelled extensively 'under concern' (under the direction of the Spirit) preaching and enlivening communities as they went.

Those who followed the Light gained a sense of freedom from outward authorities and external forms in religious and social matters: 'Your teacher is within you; look not forth.'[19] For George Fox, everything was to be tested by the Truth of one's inward guide. The teaching of priests and preachers was unreliable, reason was inadequate, and even scripture was insufficient until read by the Light of the inward guide who had inspired the scriptures in the first place.

> I was to direct people to the Spirit that gave forth the Scriptures,
> by which they might be led into all Truth, and so up to Christ and
> God, as they had been who gave them [the Scriptures] forth. And
> I was to turn them to the grace of God, and to Truth in the heart,
> which came by Jesus.[20]

Interpreting the Light Within

It is easy for twentieth-century ears to hear a modern individualism in George Fox's message which would accord an absolute sovereignty to personal inspiration. To understand reports of the spiritual experiences of early Friends we need to understand also the theological premises through which they came to terms with their experience.

Friends interpreted their powerful experiences wholly in the images and context of Christian scriptures. They were especially fond of passages in the books of the Hebrew prophets, the Pauline epistles and the gospel of John which spoke of the sacred relationship between God and God's people. A great theme of waiting-in-hope runs through the scripture texts Friends loved: God is with us, yet we are still in darkness; the reign of God is coming, yet the reign of God has already begun. Friends' interpretation of scripture about this present yet coming God took an audacious and unorthodox leap: for them the time of waiting had ended and the full and perfect relationship between God and God's people had been realised.

All of Friends' contemporaries expected that at the end of the world Christ would return and God's reign would then begin in glory. Some of their contemporaries lived in anticipation that this time would be very soon. Early Friends went a step further. Inspired by their experience of the Light Within, they believed that Christ had already returned to teach his people himself, to be their priest, their shepherd, their ruler and their judge. These activities of the glorious Christ would not mimic the ways of the world, a supernatural variant of good government, but would inwardly transform each person. The glorious 'Day of the Lord' had dawned, Christ's empowering rule was spreading across the world through the hearts of those who found him within and lived accordingly. The extent of the renewal George Fox had seen was nothing short of the restoration of the innocence and holiness of the first creation, for the individual and for the whole world:

> And the Lord showed me that such as were faithful to him in the power and the light of Christ, should come up into that state in which Adam was before he fell.[21]

In this cosmic view of the restored creation, inward mystical experiences were not a private concern but a sign that the individual had been gathered into a community of God's people.

> [We] are of the household of God, built up together a spiritual house, whose builder and maker is God.[22]

Thus, from its first days, Quakerism understood itself as a prophetic community with a mission to the world. Those inspired by the divine Spirit to speak or act could forth-tell (not foretell) the Truth of God for the present moment. The prophetic word was given not primarily for the individual but for the benefit of others: those in 'the ocean of darkness' who needed to hear the Truth for the first time, and those who had already responded but who needed to be encouraged or 'built up in the Life'. Those Friends who were particularly gifted with prophetic voices became the ministers of the new movement,

Wholly devoted to the work of the ministry, to which were we ordained of God.[23]

The guidance of the Light was matched by divine power to live a perfect Christian life where inward religion and outward religion would correspond. How one lived became a reflection of the inward transformation. Friends anchored their spirituality on two points: ongoing transcendent experience of the inward guide, and application of this guidance to daily life – right down to details of dress, shopping, speech, livelihood, spouse, and manners.

Turning to the Light and being transformed was available to everyone but was not a human ability. The Light Within was not one's conscience but the presence of the risen Christ (also commonly called The Seed, The Christ Within, and The Inward Light of Christ). The spiritual life was seen in terms of relationship between the person and the divine. George Fox exhorted Friends:

> So be wise and keep your first love. Break not wedlock with the Lord Jesus Christ.[24]

Following the example of the ministry of Jesus, the preaching of early Friends was not aimed at the learned or the good. Quaker spirituality required submission to the divine guide, and giving up reliance on one's human abilities and gifts. Describing the inward, non-intellectual approach required of anyone seeking spiritual renewal, George Fox said in 1652:

> After thou seest thy thoughts, and the temptations, do not think, but submit; and then power comes. Stand still in that which shows and discovers; and then doth strength immediately come. And stand still in the Light, and submit to it, and the other will be hush'd and gone; and then content comes.[25]

George Fox and the Seekers

The mystical experiences of George Fox marked the beginning of the spirituality of Friends. However, it has always been clear that George Fox was not unique in his spirituality, but an eminent member of a community experiencing an outbreak of mysticism. Some of those who joined George Fox had already experienced a spiritual illumination similar to his. Early followers were never George Fox's 'adherents', but were already spiritual 'finders' in their own right because, 'by the like immediate way, as George Fox himself, [they] were convinced in their minds'.[26]

The spiritual independence of early Friends was congruent with George Fox's emphasis that the true teacher was within, not without. Quakerism swept the north of England with bushfire speed, and put over sixty competent and powerful Quaker leaders into the missionary field in a few years. The authority of early Quaker preachers did not rest on George Fox's endorsement of them but on the prophetic call by their inward guide to participate in the Quaker mission. Like George Fox, they understood their role to be prophetic; they felt personally called by God to deliver a divine message to God's people.

In 1652 George Fox went to preach in Westmoreland, where Quakerism was to become a coherent spiritual community, with the capacity and determination to transmit its inward experiences to others. In isolated and independent-minded parts of northern England, some disillusioned Puritans, singly or in congregations, had left mainstream religion finding it empty. Known as separatists and also called 'Seekers'[27], these people did not have an overall group identity. They wanted their church communities to be Spirit-led and alive as in the days of the early church. Unsure how to become such a community through human effort, they gathered and waited in silence until God made clear what they should do.

Many Seekers felt that George Fox's message was the 'farther Manifestation' they had been awaiting.[28] Their name suggested they had been people with questions. In applying George Fox's preaching to their own rich experience, they became people with answers. North-country villagers had been accustomed to group decision-making in agricultural matters, so Seeker village congregations from this area were instinctively participatory and self-governing.[29] They eschewed prepared sermons, sacraments and rituals, instead holding unstructured worship, waiting in silence for prayer or witnessing as anyone was moved by the Spirit. With George Fox's encouragement they realised that their communities were full of the power of the returned Christ. Ordinary people could live holy lives now if they turned to the Light, collectively recreating the early Church in which everyone should participate as they were inspired, men and women, learned and illiterate.

Seeker groups had gifted preachers and leaders, and their congregations brought to Quakerism the seeds of a spiritual organisation which used corporate inward guidance to direct worship and daily life. They strengthened the corporate sense of Quakerism, giving individuals' powerful inward experiences a context in a worshipping community. Foremost among the corporate practices taken up by Quakerism from the Seeker groups was the practice of worshipping in silence.

Quakerism transposed a new meaning into silent worship. Silent worship began as a Seeker protest against the futility of human initiatives toward God. In Quakerism it became an expression of the worshippers' confidence that God's word would be heard. The outward form was the same, but Quaker silence became a sign that Christ had returned and was teaching his people himself, without the need for human intermediaries. Early Friends saw in their form of worship and organisation the vehicle by which the 'end time' rule of the returned Christ was being revealed and accomplished.[30]

The end of seeking

The founding generation of Quaker prophets were driven by their experience of a power beyond ordinary reality as they had previously known it, to a 'new life' in which spiritual meaning and spiritual power were the touchstones. They felt their search for ultimate meaning had ended. They had found 'Truth', a matter not only of inward and otherworldly comforts, but a detailed recipe for living a fulfilled life.

3

A great multitude to be gathered: the expansion of Quakerism

Many spiritual movements flourished and faded in seventeenth-century England. To explain the anomalous survival of Quakerism we must look beyond the founding influence of George Fox and the powerful experiences of his early Seeker companions, to their corporate vision of their community as the true church with a universal mission.

Friends felt related to one another by the bonds of fellowship laid down by Luke in Acts. In imitation of Jesus' disciples, they travelled in pairs to announce the reign of God to others. The power and energy of early Friends swept England and other parts of the world in a great spiritual renewal and Quakerism expanded rapidly.

Quaker successes provoked persecution from church and state, and ill-treatment from members of the public. Friends began to wonder how to keep the expanding Quaker community cohesive as it stretched across the world. Their opponents were ready to use the public disgrace of James Nayler in 1656 to discredit Quakers, and Friends became aware that some personal inspirations could endanger the group. They sought ways to resolve the unavoidable conflict between conserving the group and acknowledging the prophetic authority of inspired individuals.

Growth and persecution

In 1654 the Quaker push, known as the 'Valiant Sixty', moved out of the north of England to all parts of the country.[31] Their enthusiastic preaching and proselytising rapidly expanded the movement. The provocative way in which they delivered their message often prompted official reprisals and persecution.

Many travelling ministers suffered imprisonment and even death. The extent and severity of persecution of Quakers in England varied according to regional prejudices and the current pressures on the national government. Mainstream religionists had little reason to approve of them since they interrupted sermons, corrected preachers from the pews, denounced the established church as corrupt and refused to pay tithes to support 'hireling priests'. Even more scandalous, Friends defended the right of women to teach and preach. Puritans' consternation at women's preaching made persecution more extreme, but Quaker women's ministry became a key symbol of the new order that Quakers proclaimed.

Quaker enthusiasm

The Quaker evangelising style of harsh words and controversial actions was consistent with what early Friends had experienced of the Light Within, what they believed and how they lived. Their behaviour seems strange and outlandish to us but can tell us a great deal about the motivation and power of early Friends' spirituality.

Convinced that the 'end time' of the world had already come, early Quaker preachers saw themselves as God's prophets in a new age. Their message was urgent: imminent judgement and the restoration of God's reign on earth was at hand and everyone had to choose as a matter of life or death.

We know from their journals that ministers often found the task of preaching the message they were given, and the signs they felt led to perform, extremely embarrassing or difficult, but Friends were faithful to their leadings. They enacted 'signs' for unbelievers like the signs of biblical prophets: a woman Friend broke a pitcher before Parliament, a man Friend carried a lit candle to the pulpit of a local priest, and many wore sackcloth and ashes in public. The most widely used sign was 'going naked' to witness to the unconverted as the prophet Isaiah had done in Jerusalem.

Friends' understanding of the Light Within gave them a measure of detachment from the outcome of their preaching. Their task was to be faithful to their message; their preaching or sign was an opportunity for those who saw it to respond positively to the grace of God testifying within themselves. They were often met with public antagonism and treated with great cruelty[32]; for them this did not measure the rightness of a sign or preaching, but the hardness of people's hearts.

Quaker preaching applied spiritual insights to everyday life. Friends brought together inward and outward religion in a way that disconcerted their contemporaries. They condemned waste on 'fripperies' when others were in need; they denounced favouritism in the courts and the use of dishonest weights and measures among traders. Quakers particularly irked civil authorities by turning their court appearances into an opportunity to preach, and by refusing to swear oaths because this implied two standards of truthfulness. They quickly became known as 'a peculiar people'. It is not surprising that many thought them dangerous anarchists and a disruptive influence in society.[33]

Quaker preachers' extreme words and actions led many contemporaries to accuse them of insanity, immorality, or possession by evil spirits. In reality, these enthusiastic preachers usually lived sane and well-ordered lives apart from their religious activities.[34] Their testimonies were motivated by a sense of intimacy with the divine whose guidance they felt bound to follow. However, saintly and disciplined private lives were not at all obvious when a Quaker preacher stripped naked in public as a religious sign.

Becoming a Quaker

New Quaker meetings usually began with the visit of travelling Quaker ministers to an area. They preached wherever a crowd could hear them, in the open air, or in a church or chapel, hijacking a sermon to draw attention to their message. If people were interested, ministers held 'threshing meetings', usually of an evening, to teach and preach and debate with supporters and opponents. During this process, some of those attending would be 'convinced' of the truth of the Quaker message. Ministers would gather these 'tender souls' together and hold meetings for worship with them, which often continued for several hours, sometimes one person preaching spontaneously for over an hour.

The rhetorical style of Quaker preachers presupposed that people would not be convinced by the words of the preacher but by the testimony of God responding within the listener.[35] The recognition of divine action, autonomous within each person, was the basis on which a new Quaker meeting would be formed.

The spiritual awakening offered by the Quaker message had wide appeal and convincements crossed boundaries of class and education. No formal provisions granted or withheld membership to new Friends, and much is sometimes made of this today. However, the outward 'signs' new Quakers gave of their beliefs created an instant Quaker identity in public. Friends were recognised by their simplicity of dress, plainness of speech and their distaste for empty social formalities. Once an individual decided to live by the convincement experience, and keep the testimonies, a new way of life began, irrespective of social status. Thomas Ellwood, newly come to Quakers, told how his new allegiance to Friends was recognised by acquaintances from Oxford in 1659 when he did not remove his hat, or bow in greeting.

> At length, [one] clapping his hand, in a familiar way, upon my shoulder, and smiling on me, said, 'What, Tom, a Quaker!' To which I readily, and cheerfully answered, 'Yes, a Quaker'. And as the words passed out of my mouth I felt joy spring in my heart, for I rejoyced that I had not been drawn out by them into a compliance with them, and that I had the strength and boldness given me to confess myself to be one of that despised people.[36]

The basis of Quaker unity

Being noticeably different from their surrounding culture helped early Friends to form their close bonds within the Quaker group. Quakers exhibited high levels of discipline and loyalty under persecution, and their testimonies led them to treat everyone equally, without reference to class, education or gender.

However the real unity of a Quaker group lay in their spiritual bond: Friends recognised in one another their own transcendent experience of divine intimacy and shared it together during the meeting for worship. Meeting regularly refreshed the individual's personal experience of the divine and confirmed the corporate commitment of the worshipping community. Robert Barclay, writing in 1676, testifies to the cumulative significance of the repeated experience of the Quaker meeting:

>...when I came into the silent assemblies of God's people, I felt a secret power among them, which touched my heart; and as I gave way to it I found the evil weakening in me and the good raised up; and so I became thus knit and united unto them, hungering more and more after the increase of this power and life whereby I might feel myself perfectly redeemed.[37]

The group's life

Believing that Christ had returned to rule his people himself, Quaker communities felt that every aspect of their lives ought to conform to the Way of God as established by Christ. To this end, local Quaker groups cared for their members in matters of faith, worship and the conduct of daily life. They ensured that their meetings for worship were held in 'right ordering', equipped ministers from their meeting for travel in the ministry, and held 'meetings for business' to regulate their affairs. They offered pastoral care to those who were in prison or left destitute through fines for non-payment of tithes, supported new members, and made alternative provisions for Quaker marriages and burials. Often a meeting's first concern was a burial site, because Quakers, who did not practise baptism, could not be buried in consecrated ground.

Meetings to regulate group affairs mirrored meetings for worship. The silent waiting to allow God's will to guide them was another occasion for the religious experience of the community. Business meetings were not in themselves the government of a Quaker group, but the vehicle or the discipline by which the divine guide ('Christ the head') ruled the group directly. Believing that the divine will would be revealed, Friends expected unity to be the outcome of their business meeting.

>Friends are not to meet like a company of people about town or parish business... but to wait upon the Lord.[38]

The strength of the decentralised organisation of the earliest Quaker meetings lay in their autonomy, flexibility and promotion of local leadership. Their weakness lay in the risks of isolation, individualism and fragmentation. Threads were woven between far-flung Quaker groups by 'travelling ministers'. The term 'ministry' encompassed the overall care members took of one another but referred particularly to vocal ministry within the meeting for worship, when someone was inspired with words to nourish the spiritual life of the meeting as a whole. 'Ministers' were men and women who felt a divine call or 'leading' to a ministry of preaching and leadership which served their home meeting but often took them far beyond it to other countries.[39]

Despite local autonomy, Quaker meetings generally held common values, conformed to group testimonies, and practised common forms of worship and decision-making. The mix of group cohesion and local independence marked the beginning of later Quaker structures which would try to codify both principles.

Moral discipline, a beginning of corporate authority

One area which illustrated the early Quaker blend of liberty and authority was the task of the local meeting to watch over the conduct of their members, alert for 'disorderly walkers' among them, that is, for immoral behaviour. For early Quakers the personal authority of divine guidance was never an absolute value: inspiration could not overturn the requirements of a virtuous life. History had put the option clearly before early Friends in the form of a contemporary religious movement known as the Ranters. Ranters felt they had been restored to holiness in Christ, therefore all behaviour, moral or immoral, became virtuous. Quakers distanced themselves from the Ranters by insisting that attending to the Light Within led one to live righteously, without sin. In this context, early Quaker meetings were not indulgent of moral lapses among their members and disassociated themselves from behaviour which could fit critics' claims that Quakers were 'secret Ranters' and therefore immoral.

Growth toward a corporate Quaker spirituality was incremental. In 1653 William Dewsbury wrote to a meeting suggesting that a few 'seasoned' Friends should be appointed to oversee the group.[40] The letter indicated two things about a Quaker meeting at this time. First, small groups were looking for more support, advice and discipline in their life together. They felt an obligation to assist one another to live a more perfect Christian life. Second, William Dewsbury's letter, and others from around the same period, make it clear that even the strongest advice from leaders in the movement was offered to, not forced upon, meetings which were autonomous.

The dilemma of individual inspiration

Friends recognised that anyone who tried to follow divine inspirations needed to distinguish between divine guidance and aberrant impulses in oneself: 'vain imaginings', as George Fox called them. The unstable, the stressed and the gullible were particularly susceptible in the emotional and enthusiastic atmosphere of early Quakerism, but Friends were reluctant 'to crush whatever might be good in the most tormenting experiences'.[41]

Although moral lapses among members had been readily and severely disciplined, an individual's religious enthusiasms were generally permitted to run free. The weakness in respecting the authenticity of all leadings was made plain one rainy afternoon in October 1656. At the height of millenarian expectations among extreme religious groups, James Nayler, one of the most influential Quaker leaders in London, performed a sign on the streets of Bristol which was to have far-reaching effects on the formation of the Religious Society of Friends.

James Nayler re-enacted Christ's entry into Jerusalem. A group of six of his followers from London led him into Bristol on horseback shouting 'Hosannah' and 'Holy, holy, holy', spreading their cloaks before the horse. Local Bristol Quakers tried to dissociate themselves from the spectacle. When James Nayler came to trial, his guilt rested on the question whether he was enacting a sign of the return of Christ or whether he was claiming to be Christ himself returning. For James Nayler the distinction was clear: his action was a sign; but it was not clear for some of his followers. Referring to the evidence offered by Dorcas Erbury, James Nayler's biographer noted:

To the more open-minded and better informed of those under whose jurisdiction the case would ultimately fall, her evidence was not so damning as a proof of events, but as an example of the potential danger of sophisticated doctrines in simple hands.[42]

The Parliamentary debate over James Nayler's case generated a lot of adverse publicity and damaged Friends' reputation with the public. It also eroded support for religious toleration for all Nonconformists, confirming the view of many Puritans that religious toleration was dangerous, ill-advised and likely to encourage excesses. The severity of the punishment meted out to James Nayler showed that the national authorities had become alarmed at the successes of the new religious radicals known as Quakers.

The events involving James Nayler had damaged unity among Friends. His own motivation in enacting this sign is not clear, but behind it were two momentous issues for the Quaker movement: how to assess the authenticity of individuals' leadings, and how to exercise authority appropriately in a movement in which everyone felt directly inspired by God.

How to assess individuals' inspirations had been James Nayler's problem for some months before the Bristol ride. He had become prominent in the Quaker mission in London. Among his admirers were radical London Friends who took an extreme view of human perfectibility. James Nayler, they thought, was the most perfect in the movement and should therefore be leader.[43] His advocates praised him in extravagant and apocalyptic terms, disrupting meetings if prominent Quakers other than James Nayler spoke. Tactics that Friends had used against other religious groups were effective in disrupting their own meetings too, and London meetings were in disarray. After an initial attempt, James Nayler seemed reluctant to restrain his promoters in case he was interfering with an authentic, divine inspiration. Other Friends in London tried to discipline the group to no avail. James Nayler's supporters countered reprimands with the claim that God willed them to do these things.

George Fox pressured James Nayler to control the disruptive group.[44] Perhaps over-scrupulous about trying to find and follow

God's will, James Nayler seemed to give in to a paralysing depression. Personal conflict between George Fox and James Nayler made the situation worse. In two unedifying episodes they struggled over George Fox's authority to discipline James Nayler. James Nayler insulted George Fox by keeping his hat on during the latter's prayer, and in an extraordinary incident the following day, George Fox asked James Nayler to kiss his foot 'because the Lord God moved me to slight him and to set the power of God over him'.[45] George Fox's behaviour in trying to push James Nayler to this kind of submission seemed the antithesis of the spiritual equality of persons that the movement had espoused. Whatever the extent to which the Bristol incident originated in the power struggle of the two Quaker leaders, ultimately James Nayler 'allowed himself to be used by unbalanced people whom he originally did not have the courage to discipline'.[46]

Walking forward more carefully

Despite the tragic elements of James Nayler's story, his fall was a catalyst.[47] The fledgling Quaker community had seen the dangers of autonomous individual inspirations in less steady souls. Some check on overzealous individuals' spiritual 'leadings' was needed for the movement to survive. The growth of Quaker structures would no longer be left to chance, the prophetic authority of the individual's inspiration would be gradually curbed by the authority of the group.

> ...while Nayler's fall prejudiced the work of Friends in various ways... its most lasting result was good, for it effectively warned the Quaker leaders of the perils attending the over-emphasis which they had laid on the infallibility of the life possessed by the Spirit of Christ. Henceforth they walked more carefully, heedful of the special temptations which beset the path of spiritual enthusiasm.[48]

4

Settling the flock:
stabilising the Quaker Way

At the end of the James Nayler episode, the fragile but expanding Quaker movement faced the dilemma of every ecstatic religious group: how to survive beyond the first generation, avoiding fragmentation as enthusiasts spun off under the influence of disparate inspirations. The challenge was to bridle transcendent experiences without repressing them. Friends' solution to this dilemma would be one of the most creative in the history of religious organisations. The authority of an individual's inspiration would be maintained, but tested by spiritual processes in which the whole community could participate. Since every matter was a matter for finding God's will and for inspiration, there would be no distinction between sacred and secular life, and the fellowship of members was strengthened accordingly. Communities would be local, intimate, and linked with others in a hierarchy of meetings, not of persons.

After James Nayler's disgrace George Fox emerged as the unquestioned leader of the Quaker movement, and used his authority to settle communities feeling the effects of the Nayler turmoil. George Fox wrote three epistles urging internal reconciliation, a more profound sense of the Spirit during meetings for worship, and that more experienced Friends should guide those in the group who 'go beyond their measure'.[49]

George Fox also expanded a system of men's quarterly meetings to cover the south of the country as well as the north, and began general meetings at Skipton. These wider gatherings were advisory and implementation of any policy was still strictly a local matter, but they prefigured the way Friends' meetings would regulate spiritual inspirations of individuals. It had become clear that a formal organisation might better curb individual excesses destructive to the group, and a more cohesive group could more effectively document and resist State persecution of its members. With these good intentions Friends rapidly changed their organisational style from a loose network emphasising the infallibility of inspiration, to a highly disciplined and coherent body, unchanged and stable for almost two centuries.

Toward 'Gospel Order'

The Restoration of King Charles in 1660 finally ended Reformation hopes for the Rule of the Saints. Prior to 1660 Friends' sufferings had been intense but spasmodic and regional. After the Restoration, persecution of Quakers became national policy. In 1662 the Quaker Act outlawed Quaker gatherings, and thousands of Friends were imprisoned for meeting openly. The Conventicle Act of 1664 extended this to apply to all Noncomformists. The Second Conventicle Act of 1670 was intended to enrich state coffers and bankrupt Nonconformists. Trials were held without a jury and conviction could be made on the word of an informer. Heavy fines, imposed on anyone hosting or preaching at an outlawed meeting, would be divided equally among the state, the poor and the informer. Informing on Nonconformists became an industry, with some informers travelling from county to county in search of profit.

The authorities underestimated Quaker persistence under persecution When all Nonconformist gatherings were made illegal, many groups resorted to the pragmatic but less inspiring practice of 'house-creeping', that is, meeting in private homes under the guise of a social event. Only the Baptists and the Quakers maintained public meetings. Inspired by this faithfulness, many joined Friends during the years of persecution.

By the time persecution of Nonconformists officially ended with the Toleration Act of 1689, over 15,000 Quakers had suffered imprisonment or other punishments during the Restoration period and at least 450 had died as a result of their imprisonment.[50]

Divisions over the authority of personal inspiration

Beleaguered by persecution, Quaker communities tried to care for new members even when most ministers and experienced Friends were in prison. They were also haunted by shadows from the James

Nayler controversy. James Nayler had been reconciled to the Quakers before his death in 1660 but a new threat to unity arose in 1661, involving many of those who had supported James Nayler. John Perrot, an influential Friend, pushed the testimony against outward forms to extremes. He wanted everything, including the time and place of meeting for worship, to be spontaneously guided by the Spirit.

The basis of John Perrot's position was that only the inward attitude of the person counted before God. An individual's inspirations of the moment had the full force of divine authority. By severing the connection between inward faith and outward forms, John Perrot's position allowed conformity to the outward religious requirements of the State, providing one did not conform inwardly. In a period of intense persecution this was a seductive doctrine, and gained support among some Friends.

John Perrot died in Barbados in 1665, but the individualistic style of inward Quakerism he had promoted did not die with him. It marked a turning point in the formation of Quaker spirituality. When George Fox was released from prison in September 1666, he found Friends fraught by persecution and divided among themselves. Division, loss of leadership through imprisonment, and the absence of corporate authority sparked a profound crisis in the Quaker movement. The time would have been opportune for George Fox to institutionalise his own position as leader of the movement. Instead, he created a sustainable organisation, which he called 'Gospel order', to provide leadership and regulate church life, while at the same time retaining the primacy of religious experience in Quaker life.

Gospel order as a system of church government

Despite being in extremely poor health after his imprisonment, George Fox began an arduous visitation to all the meetings of England, reconciling dissidents and establishing a superstructure of decision-making meetings. Between 1667 and 1674 George Fox used his personal influence to establish Gospel order, whereby personal infallibility through divine guidance was to be complemented and tested by corporate discernment of the divine will. Gospel order used the essential spiritual experience of the Quaker community as a system of government. Meetings conducted business by gathering together in silence and waiting for unity and divine inspiration to be made known among them. The authority of the meeting rested with the Spirit, not with the people.

> Keep your meetings in the Power of God... And when Friends have finished their business, sit down and continue a while quietly and wait upon the Lord to feel him. And go not beyond the Power, but keep in the Power by which God almighty may be felt among you... For the Power of the Lord will work through all, if... you follow it.[51]

By the 1670s the Quaker movement had been sufficiently stabilised to be called the 'Religious Society of Friends'. The Society was constituted with a hierarchy of meetings at district ('Monthly'), regional ('Quarterly') and national ('Yearly') levels, to which experienced Friends were sent by their meetings, thus engaging in corporate service the best spiritual leadership of meetings all across the country. Meetings' business included the relief of the poor, the recording of persecution and suffering among Friends, and the discipline of the group.

Developments toward central control

The Society was rapidly formalised. Quarterly Meetings were still advisory in nature, but were influential due to their efficiency and the high status of the experienced Friends chosen to attend them. Ministers had previously had some annual meetings in London during Commonwealth days. Such meetings lapsed under persecution but after tentative beginnings in 1668, an annual national meeting of ministers and a parallel meeting of Quaker representatives from all the counties met 'to advise about the managing of the public affairs of Friends throughout the nation'.[52] London Yearly Meeting had begun.

London Yearly Meeting provided direction and focus for the Society and enabled ministers and experienced Friends, gathered from all parts of the country, to forge common understandings of the Quaker Way. Early in the 1670s two standing committees further strengthened central authority. The first (Morning Meeting) supervised and passed books for publication, and became a key body in shaping and dispersing the Quaker message. The second (Meeting for Sufferings) collected and recorded evidence about the injustices done to Friends to help lobby Parliamentarians and the legal profession.[53]

As well as recording and publishing about the Society, the London committees offered advice and recommendations to individuals and districts, especially about matters which reflected on the whole Society whose cause they propounded on a national level. In a Society where all were ostensibly equal, Friends on key committees now found their inspirations and discernments very influential in directing the life of the Society. Although autonomous, local groups lacked the overview of the London committees, and were at a disadvantage if they disagreed. The increased centralisation of London Yearly Meeting meant that inspirations from individuals or local meetings were less able to influence the whole Society.

Women's meetings: a contentious part of Gospel order

A positive consequence of the increased authority of London Yearly Meeting was that the organisation was able to institutionalise some of its radical and prophetic elements before respectability overtook them.

In the face of the Society's need to demonstrate that Quakers were not an anarchic and socially dangerous sect, Friends' testimony to the equality of women became problematic. By the 1670s many of the first generation of radical, heroic women ministers who had stirred up England with their preaching had aged or were dead from their hardships. In less radical times there was less room for women.

Faced with these shifting sentiments, George Fox felt that Gospel order required women as well as men to participate in the Society's decision-making. Separate women's meetings were set up alongside men's business meetings. The authority of the women's meetings was limited but not token: for example, they 'cleared' a couple for marriage, and controlled extensive funds for the relief of Friends and their families in need. Most power rested with men's meetings, but setting up women's meetings still provoked discord among some Friends. Many men did not want women to participate in the business of the Society.

The practice of gender equality among Friends had never been wholehearted. Some held that woman's equality was spiritual, and man should remain the head in temporal matters. Depending on local sentiments, women's participation in meetings varied from district to district. Yearly Meeting was still encouraging some local meetings to set up their women's meeting seventy-five years after the first women's meeting was established, and London Yearly Meeting (men only) had no parallel women's meeting until 1784.

In setting up women's meetings, central authority created a place for women's inspirations to be heard. These inspirations would otherwise have been lost in many local meetings as women were increasingly silenced. Although the Society undoubtedly lost a great deal of vigour through increased centralisation, it would be a mistake to overlook the fact that central intervention in the affairs of local meetings kept the inspiration base wider than it would have been if those who opposed the role of women in Gospel order had had their way.

Conflict over Gospel order

Two well-respected northern Friends, John Story and John Wilkinson, were particularly opposed to the changes George Fox had initiated. They had been among the 'Valiant Sixty' and remained influential in the Society, especially in the north.

Their objections to the provisions of Gospel order were ostensibly to defend individual inspiration. They argued that the group did not have the authority to bind the inspiration of the individual, even on long-standing corporate testimonies. They felt that a meeting had no authority to 'draw up papers of condemnation' against a wayward Friend, unless that Friend had owned that s/he had deserved such condemnation; nor should a meeting do more than try to persuade Friends to keep the testimony against tithes; finally, Friends should be free to meet secretly if the Spirit so inspired them, and thus avoid informers and the resulting heavy fines. During the intense persecution of the 1670s the idea that a personal 'leading' could exempt one from the hardships of communal testimonies attracted some Friends, but troubled others deeply.

While claiming to support the free inspirations of all Friends, some of John Wilkinson's and John Story's objections actually seemed to restrict rather than liberate individuals. John Wilkinson and John Story vigorously protested any authoritative inspiration coming from the newly established Women's meetings, particularly in their role to 'clear' a couple for marriage before the matter was brought to the men's meeting. They also opposed the customary free participation in business meeting of any Friend who happened to be present, insisting that only appointed delegates ought 'to have a voice', and anyone else with anything to offer 'might declare their message and withdraw'. Finally, they wanted to restrain Friends who felt inspired to make supportive noise ('sound') during vocal ministry in worship. In the light of reports of the time, this custom must have been irritating but wanting to restrain this inspiration among Friends somewhat detracted from John Wilkinson's and John Story's spirited defence of individual inspiration on other issues.

This assessment of John Story's and John Wilkinson's objections suggests that the eventual separation of their faction from the Society in 1675 was not about the absolute authority of individual inspiration. Rather they were contesting who had authority over individual inspiration of members: an autonomous local group, or a local group subject to a central authority. In practice, the Wilkinson-Story faction wanted to exclude some of its members from the participation, inspiration and authority accorded them by the central organisation.

Outcomes of centralisation

The Wilkinson–Story separation has been represented as a final chapter in the demise of the local and autonomous Quaker meetings and the final defence of individual inspiration against corporate discipline.[54] The separatists did support regional authority against national authority, but within those narrower confines their intentions were clear: to enforce their own kind of conformity, especially on women Friends. The tides of conformity were flowing at both regional and national levels.

Meetings became preoccupied with supervising daily life to ensure that members did not infringe Quaker custom in dress, speech, behaviour, lifestyle or occupation. Transcendent experiences would now conform to the meeting's norms of content, imagery and occasion. The very measures zealous Friends took to protect the Society would in the end produce a 'self-contained, introspective sect, out of touch with the world that it should be conquering for the Kingdom of God'.[55] Friends accepted the authority of communal discernment over the inspirations of the individual, and accepted spiritual leadership from the higher level meetings and London committees. An atmosphere of compliance was further encouraged by the high status and efficiency of ministers, elders and others who represented the body of Friends on national committees and at Yearly Meeting. Turning outward for spiritual nourishment or inspiration, even reading of the Bible, became suspect as Friends relied on the inward guide they found in themselves and in the will of the community as expressed in 'the discipline'. Michael Sheeran summarised Friends' loss:

> The personally-felt leadings of the Spirit, whether experienced in private or in the local meeting, were supplemented and, to a large extent, supplanted by the directions received from higher structural entities.[56]

Stabilised Quakerism: a difficult but rich legacy

At the close of the seventeenth century, as persecution ended with the Declaration of Indulgences (1688) and Act of Toleration (1689), London Yearly Meeting had achieved a great deal. By political lobbying, dispersal of accurate legal information to Friends for their defence when arrested, and tight group discipline, Quakers had established a place for their anarchic ideas as a permissible, if not respectable, alternative in English national life. By 1696 an Affirmation Act allowed Friends to affirm rather than swear an oath before the courts. Within fifty years the radical fringe movement of the 'Children of the Light' had been transformed within and without into the respectable, increasingly prosperous, Religious Society of Friends. In sociological terms Quakerism had been stabilised.

The errors of eighteenth-century Quakerism were many, and they are easy for their successors to disdain. Closed off from the world, inward looking, the quietist century of the Quaker community is best remembered now for its negative qualities. Ministry was often dead, usually confined to recorded ministers whose prophetic words were lost or over-regulated by too vigilant elders. The prohibition on marrying non-Quakers evicted many vibrant young Friends from the community. Being a worthy Friend was too easily judged by conformity to the Quaker 'particularities' of speech and dress rather than by the power of a life faithful to inward guidance Financial success increased the likelihood that one's contributions to the Society would be heard, since a voluntary ministry usually required independent means.

Modern criticism of the quietist period of Quakerism usually focusses on their preoccupation with policing the outward forms of their corporate religious life. It would be simplistic to equate the stable period of Quaker life with stagnation. Friends of the period well understood that there was an eternity of difference between keeping the outward forms and the inward experience of being a Friend. Cheerful and rebellious Betsy Gurney, a birthright Friend, who conformed outwardly, in most details except her red shoes, had a powerful religious experience and was convinced. That night she confided to her diary, 'I am to become a Quaker'. She did and the world now knows her as Elizabeth Fry. The story of Samuel Bownas is well known and loved among Friends. He was 'but a traditional Quaker' until he knew the power for himself.[57] Another birthright Friend commented:

> ...I saw closely in that Day (when I came to dye) that unless I came to be acquainted with the same Power that had wrought a Change and Alteration in my dear Parents... I should be miserable and undone forever.[58]

We Friends are here in this time because key elements of Quaker spirituality, with vital potential, were treasured and retained through years of quietism. These elements were preserved in the very structures which had subsumed them, ensuring their accessibility to future generations of Friends.

Just as the worst of nineteenth-century French Catholic piety was able to produce Teresa of Lisieux, so eighteenth-century Quakerism produced John Woolman. These graced individuals attained wholeness/ holiness not by sidestepping the excesses of their respective religious cultures, but by finding and living out the fundamental charism or genius of their tradition with creativity and power.

Eighteenth-century Quakerism clung to and lived out the early Friends' testimony of 'realised eschatology', that is they understood their isolated community to embody the power of the returned and victorious Christ. This testimony had made the first Friends tireless missionaries. It turned their successors inward, staying apart in their calling to be God's faithful community. Preserving this Quaker vision of realised eschatology was the most important factor in keeping the Quaker Way accessible to later generations of Friends. Although the prophetic task and prophetic power may have been domesticated to warm only a small family hearth, its raging spiritual potential had been safeguarded and maintained.

The diverse branches of Quakerism continued to believe that the will and guidance of the divine Spirit can be known to everyone. Quaker organisation relied on the Spirit speaking to, directing and challenging the community as a whole. In this organisational atmosphere, Friends, even at their most rigid, had an inbuilt openness to being surprised by the Spirit, a capacity for the unexpected. Unpredictable, beyond human control, disturbing, the constant possibility of spiritual experience was inherent in being a Friend in any age.

Despite the superstructure of Yearly Meeting and its influential committees, local meetings remained the roots of power in Quaker organisation. They appointed Friends as ministers, elders and as representatives to higher level meetings. Quaker leaders became leaders because their local meetings had found them worthy and useful in service. Ministers were responsible to their home meetings, even when they travelled far from home. Friends became 'ministers' when their prophetic and preaching gifts were formally recognised by their own meeting and they were recorded as ministers in the minutes.

And all that be public ministers, if unknown, that pass up and down the countries and to other nations, [let] them... have a certificate from their Meetings, where such persons are known and all their practices are looked into.[59]

Most ministers travelled extensively, and in this way scarce human resources were shared and exchanged and the fellowship of local meetings was supplemented by a stream of experienced and inspiring contacts. Without professional ministers, Quaker spirituality, from its inception to the twentieth century, relied on a system of intervisitation by travelling lay ministers to sustain small, isolated Quaker groups. They effectively nourished and unified a vast network of Friends. American Quaker Rufus Jones (1863-1948) described his own childhood experience of travelling ministers:

> Among the many influences which went to form and determine my early life, I should give a large place to the visits of itinerant Friends who came to us from far and near. It was a novel custom, this constant interchange of gifted ministers... We were isolated, and without this contact with the great world we should have had a narrow ingrowing life, but through this splendid spiritual cross-fertilisation, we had a chance to increase and improve the quality of our life and thought...
>
> Our little local group also had its outgoing stream of itinerant ministry. ... [The minister] rose to say that for a long time the Lord had been calling her to a service in a distant Yearly Meeting... and now she had come to ask Friends to release her for this service. One after another the Friends would 'concur in this concern', and the blessing of the Lord would be invoked upon the messenger who was going forth.
>
> Some of these occasions were of a heavenly sort, and the voices of strong men choked in tears as a beloved brother or sister was equipped and set free. From this little meeting heralds went out to almost every part of the world, and the act of liberation was something never to be forgotten, and only to be surpassed by the deep rejoicing which stirred the same company when the journey was over and 'the minutes were returned'.[60]

5

'Quaker caution and love of detail gone to seed' [61]: destabilisation and breakdown of the Quaker tradition

A period of stability in a religious organisation, according to the Fitz–Cada model, may last decades or centuries, ending when established customs and procedures stop working for the group and new questions challenge old certainties. When an organisation can no longer meet their needs, members become dissatisfied and hunger for something more meaningful. The spiritual life of such a community is experienced as outward form without inward vitality. This phase, which Raymond Fitz and Lawrence Cada called 'breakdown', can be rapid or lingering, positive or negative in its final outcome, depending on the organisation's responses to the challenges it faces.

Breakdown in religious organisations can be stimulated by outside challenges which filter into the community's life. Organisations can also collapse inwards, unable to nourish themselves adequately or to carry the weight of their own structures. The breakdown of the stabilised phase of Quakerism was sparked by both internal and external factors. Internal factors included a serious decline of membership. Many Friends married non-Friends, and were disowned or left the Society. Few convinced Friends came to take their place during the decades of isolation. Other Friends, particularly young Friends, rebelled when meetings tried to supervise their speech, dress and behaviour.

Two forces outside nineteenth-century Quakerism heightened internal stresses and pushed the organisation into a period of breakdown. These forces were, in many ways, contrary ones: the powerful revival of Christian evangelicalism, and a growing secular (that is, non-religious) interpretation of the world and the meaning of human life.

The initial Quaker response to internal and external challenges was typical of religious organisations in crisis: an attempt to enforce existing norms more fervently. Quaker meetings all over the world tried to 'tighten the discipline'. In the United States the breakdown period meant the literal breakup of American Quakerism as Friends grappled with the challenges and opportunities confronting them, and divided when they could not agree on solutions. Schism occurred in London Yearly Meeting too, but only on a small scale for historical and geographical reasons.[62] The breakdown of stabilised Quakerism during the nineteenth century was far-reaching and Quakers' self-image was transformed. The peculiar people who had seen themselves as God's faithful remnant, safe and apart from the world, became the leading philanthropists, humanitarians and social reformers of their age.

The challenge of evangelical Christianity

Seventeenth-century Quakers offered personal, enthusiastic religious experience to everyone. By the following century Quakers were focused inward, and Methodism began a successful evangelical revival based on personal faith and direct experience of God being available to all. Soon evangelical influences were being felt even within insular Quaker communities across England and the United States. In the early 1800s influential Friends with evangelical links travelled extensively on both sides of the Atlantic, spreading evangelical theology, language and attitudes throughout the world Quaker family. Evangelicalism reached its peak in London Yearly Meeting in the 1870s.

Modern Friends of the unprogrammed tradition now tend to equate evangelical Christianity with conservative or repressive theology. But in the last century, the evangelicals were the radicals among Friends. They encouraged the closed Quaker community to be more open, promoted spiritual renewal and broke down barriers between the Society of Friends and the world. Friends came out of their isolation, attracted by refreshing spiritual experiences through devotion to Christ and reading of the Bible. Evangelical contacts also challenged Friends to be involved in 'the world' as a Christian duty, working especially for humanitarian and religious concerns such as anti-slavery, prison reform and the spread of literacy (to promote reading of the Bible). Ultimately, evangelical influences breached two Quaker structures which had kept the Society a closed community with a terminal decline in numbers. In 1861 London Yearly Meeting revised the Discipline: endogamy (marrying a fellow Quaker) and the particularities of Quaker speech and dress were no longer mandatory for English Friends. In the eighteenth century Quakers had stressed the distinctiveness of their community; the evangelical revival reminded them of the faith experience they had in common with other Protestant Christians.

Evangelicalism refreshed Friends' spirituality through scripture-based experiences of Jesus as Lord, and reawakened a sense of divine purpose in their community life. The self-nurturing function of the community flourished too. Revival gatherings restored Friends and brought in new members, particularly in the United States.

Although evangelicalism significantly enriched Quaker life, it also disturbed key features of the Quaker Way. To some extent this occurred because evangelical influences came into the Society informally, on the coattails of Friends who had found renewed spiritual energy in their evangelical encounters. Quaker meetings and gatherings became caught up in evangelical enthusiasm, and the Quaker tradition found itself ill-equipped to harmonise some evangelical views with treasured elements of the quietist tradition, such as the authority of the Inward Guide.

Evangelical Friends rightly understood that many of their views were an authentic expression of the Quaker tradition, and they read and quoted early Quaker writings to prove it. However, they selectively emphasised passages about Christ's atonement, the personal reception of grace and the authority of scripture. Evangelicals set aside the parts of the Quaker tradition they disagreed with, such as the universality of the Light. Prior to the evangelical challenge, Quaker theology and spirituality had not been substantially reformed since Robert Barclay's definitive work. His *Apology* expressed early Friends' successful synthesis of Christian biblical faith and universal salvation and which balanced individual and corporate authority.[63] Evangelical Friends rejected Robert Barclay's work.

The 1870s were the high point of evangelical Christianity's spiritual and social contributions to the life of London Yearly Meeting. By 1875 it is estimated that there were as many members of the outreach 'mission meetings' in Britain as there were Friends. Mission meetings were programmed meetings sponsored by evangelical Friends for non-Friends who would have felt 'uncomfortable' with the silence. London Yearly Meeting's commitment to the doctrinal tenets of evangelicalism remained ambivalent, and mission meetings never joined the mainstream of English Quakerism. In 1887 the Richmond Declaration was formulated in Indiana in the United States, with input from weighty English Friends, and many anticipated its endorsement by London Yearly Meeting as a credal basis for Quakerism. When it failed, the door closed rapidly on the evangelical option for English Quakerism but evangelical and quietist elements continued to exist side by side in many meetings, the implications of their propinquity unexamined.

The challenge of rationalism and science

In stepping back from the evangelical position laid down in the Richmond Declaration, English Friends reacted with Quakerly caution to the dangers of outward expression of religion. They were also attuned to the religious import of progress in modern science and rationalism at the close of the nineteenth century.

Twentieth-century Quakers would be free of the rigid disciplines of the quietist period, and free of evangelical doctrine as a basis for religious faith. Yet Friends at the turn of the century were aware that mere absence of form and content did not nourish spiritual life, and they began to explore the grounds for a contemporary faith. They turned avidly to the history and theology of early Quakerism, to new scholarship about scripture, and to secular and scientific understandings about the nature of human beings and their place in the world. Most of all Friends turned again to the foundation of the Quaker Way: their own experience as spiritual women and men in the world.

Paradigm shifts in the modern world offered Friends new ways of thinking about the origins, psychology and social habits of human beings, the creation of the world, the nature of Nature and the composition, and hence the authority, of sacred texts. At the turn of the century many people, inside and outside the Society of Friends, had intellectual or moral reservations about the dogma and practices of mainstream Christianity. Aware of this growing disillusionment with formal religion, Quakers increasingly valued their traditional caution toward dogmatic forms, and affirmed their ethical testimonies. They opened themselves fully to 'the world', as the place where God's purposes would be fulfilled and where all human beings could respond to that of God within them. Whatever the source of inspiration, modern Quakers would try to be receptive to finding God's patterns in the world.

Advances in biblical scholarship, and participation in this work by Friends such as Rendel Harris, enabled Friends with rational or ethical objections to parts of the Bible to continue to read the text as a religious document. A bloodthirsty God and Hebraic cosmology were no longer seen as revelation but as a matter of history and culture. New scholarly approaches to scripture fitted what Friends were rediscovering about their own early traditions. The pre-evangelical Quaker view that the authority of scripture resided in the Spirit, not in the text itself, was reclaimed and treasured by twentieth-century Friends. Robert Barclay's *Apology* was reprinted in new editions and belief in the universal Light was again commonly held.

In London Yearly Meeting, organisational change followed in the wake of shifting attitudes, modifying structures which had constrained and sustained the Society for so long. For example, after the promising beginnings of early Friends, the role of women had been restricted for most of the Society's history. At the turn of the century Quaker women were allowed to participate more fully in the life of the community: in 1880 separate women's and men's Yearly Meetings met in joint session for the first time; in 1896 women became part of the Yearly Meeting (that is the men's Yearly Meeting) and thus available for appointment to the influential Meeting for Sufferings. In 1907 separate women's meetings were terminated altogether since equality between men and women Friends had been achieved! In May 1918 a woman, Mary Jane Godlee, served as clerk of a London Yearly Meeting session for the first time.

Other quietist remnants were swept away during the period of breakdown, including the powerful 'Ministry Committees' of elders and ministers, the Morning Meeting which had supervised Quaker publications since the 1670s, and lifeterm eldership. Quaker structures that had operated for two centuries to promote a prophetic ministry were deemed no longer to be working.

Many early twentieth-century Friends were dedicated to the revival of powerful ministry in Quaker meetings. In 1924 business meetings stopped recording particular Friends as 'ministers'. Tony Brown noted that in taking this decision three factors seemed to be operating:

> The least of these was the current administrative untidiness of the recording process. The only practical solution with which all Friends could agree, was abolition. The second was a sense that the weight of the recorded ministers was frustrating the ministry of others. Again the line of least resistance was taken, by sweeping this difficult question under the carpet of abolition. It has not gone away, and any one of us can produce anecdotes of those who are still unable to minister because of the weighty presence of this or that Friend. The third factor, perceived as the antidote to the second, was the repetition of the principle of our common responsibility for ministry: 'We were all Ministers if true Friends'. This paper does not deny this, but proposes that it is one-sided. It overlooks the human psychology understood by the Apostle Paul, that we are all called not only to a general ministry, but that we are each gifted to special ministries (I Cor 12:28).[64]

Friends hoped the abolition of recorded ministers would free the Spirit of inspiration and service in everyone, spreading the prophetic, conserving and nurturing functions of the Society more broadly across its membership. These changes to the practice of ministry in the Society had been preceded by creative initiatives to renew its spirit, including Summer Schools, Conferences, the settlement at Woodbrooke and the inauguration of the Swarthmore Lecture. Changes to Friends' structures allowed more spiritual, intellectual and behavioural freedom to members of the Society.

Until this time Friends' structures, however obsolete and difficult, had protected and nurtured particular elements of the Quaker Way.

With the benefit of hindsight it remains to asked: were sufficient outwards forms retained, or created, to channel prophetic experience through the community, to renew it in the present and sustain it in the future?

The Australian experience

For over 100 years Australian Quakers were members of London Yearly Meeting and experienced the breakdown period of Quakerism from that distant perspective. Ongoing dependence on London Yearly Meeting is atypical of the pattern of Quaker evolution in other parts of the world. In the United States of America, groups of meetings quickly formed themselves into autonomous Yearly Meetings with responsibility for the conduct of their own affairs. Independence, substantial memberships and distance from England allowed them to develop and adapt the inherited traditions of English Quakerism to suit local conditions. Australian Quakerism had no such opportunity. It remained bound to the model of London Yearly Meeting by ties of authority, affection and, above all, by its own small numbers.

Local meetings in Australia have always been small and a long way from one another. Moreover, until becoming an independent Yearly Meeting in 1967, they were a very long way from their higher authority in Quaker structures, Yearly Meeting in London. Quaker organisation and custom had been developed to suit numerous, geographically accessible communities. When immigrant English Quakers tried to live out their valued structures and customs among small and isolated groups in Australia they created tensions in, and lost members from, their already tiny Meetings. The 1861 revision of the discipline allowing Friends to marry non-Friends was of great relief in the small and isolated populations of Quakers in Australia, where finding a partner to marry 'in' was very hard indeed. The peculiarities of Quaker customs also limited the appeal of Quakerism to the wider Australian community, restricting opportunities for growth by recruitment.

Australian allegiance to the usages of English Quakerism produced a common Quaker tradition in both countries despite the fluctuations in customs and belief over time. As a distant and tiny outpost of

London Yearly Meeting, Australian Quakerism was particularly affected by the breakdown of stabilised Quakerism in Britain. During the early part of the Australian Quaker story, the evangelical influences of London Yearly Meeting were dominant. The influential visit of English Quakers James Backhouse and George Washington Walker to Australia in the 1830s is an outstanding example of the spiritual and humanitarian achievements of evangelical Quakerism, an influence sustained by many later immigrants.[65]

Radical change began in London Yearly Meeting after the Manchester Conference in 1895. Close interpersonal links, and popular, well-attended summer schools did much to unify and reassure British Friends as entrenched structures were broken down. Australian Friends had few opportunities to participate in or be reassured by these initiatives, and the spirit and purpose of change passed many of them by. A significant number of Quaker immigrants had been alienated from their meetings prior to coming to Australia; others had felt the separation from London Yearly Meeting keenly. Whatever their views, Australian Friends could only watch from afar as the character of the religious community they had known changed dramatically. Many resisted the changes they observed and held tenaciously to more familiar ways and attitudes. For this reason, evangelical spirituality and tradition endured in pockets of Australian Quakerism long after it had ceased to dominate London Yearly Meeting.

Later Quaker immigrants to Australia from London Yearly Meeting were a different kind of Friend: non-evangelical, committed to the authority of the Light Within and ongoing revelation, involved with the world's issues, and, increasingly, 'convinced' rather than birthright. Furthermore, these Friends drew to Australian Quakerism a steady stream of new 'Friends by convincement' from local communities. Thus contemporary Australian Quakerism has a mixed heritage, with Bible-based evangelicalism surviving alongside an evolving Quaker tradition which looked both to 'the Light' of the early Friends and to the needs of the world around them as sources of authority. In the 1980s this dual heritage was made visible in the collision of two divergent traditions of Quakerism. The occasion of this conflict was the proposal to insert a supportive statement on committed relationships other than marriage into the *Handbook of Practice and Procedure* of Australia Yearly Meeting.

The development of this conflict, and its temporary resolution, (the contested section being included in an appendix to the *Handbook*) illustrated, for those who wished to read the signs, the kinds of challenges faced by the current diversity of Quakerism in Australian Yearly Meeting or London [now Britain] Yearly Meeting. These challenges were only marginally related to the presenting issues of sexual standards and morality. At the heart of the matter were the perennial Quaker tensions: between the inspiration of the individual and the discernment of the community; between the word of God in scripture, and the word of God still being spoken; between decisions at the centre of the organisation and decisions in the local group.

Toward renewal?

Australian or British Quakers can no longer assume a common Quaker view of God, humans and the world. The challenge remains to find a lasting basis for our faith, unity and our social action which takes account of the diversity and the heritage of modern Friends. A century after the process of renewal began some initiatives have been fruitful, but we are not yet a revived community. We struggle to find and to describe a satisfying spirituality for individuals and for our corporate life, and we are uncertain what to say to others who come to our meetings asking for nourishment. We have been at this turning point for a long time.

At this point it may be helpful to consider the final stage of the Fitz–Cada model, which suggests essential elements for the renewal of a religious community in a stage of transition.

6

Way will open: Quakerism in transition

The final stage in the life cycle of a religious community, according to the Fitz–Cada model, is termed 'transition'. In this last stage the majority of religious communities simply die out. Others survive at a minimal level, like the remaining Shaker and Amish communities in America. Only a small percentage of communities revive after breakdown to re-experience religious enthusiasm and pass it on to others.

A faith community in transition will rightly ask itself the regular questions of any organisation in crisis: 'What is wrong?', 'What can we do to fix it?' Faith communities which look for and accept the guidance of God in their corporate life also need to ask other questions: 'Have we been faithful to the guidance we have received?', 'Where is this crisis leading us?' The most powerful factor affecting a religious organisation's vitality will be the vigour with which its members, corporately and individually, feel united and inspired by relationship with the divine.

Religious communities in crisis often try to induce spiritual renewal through organisational change. The decision to stop recording ministers may have been, in part, this kind of response. Making structural adjustments or trying to improve communication between members may seem easier than facing our powerlessness to heal spiritual malaise by human effort, but the spiritual openness of a community to divine guidance is what will ultimately determine the success or failure of their transition.

Healing spiritual malaise within a group and initiating revival cannot be accomplished by office-holders or weighty Friends. It must be the committed task of a large section of the community, if not all of it. Transformation of a group can begin nowhere else but within each person. Willingness in many members to begin the hard work of inward transformation, without waiting for others to go first, may be the test of a community's desire and capacity to be revitalised.

How can we revitalise our community?

The renewal of a religious organisation demands that many of its members be willing to risk being led by the Spirit. The Fitz–Cada model identified three hallmarks of renewed communities: profound renewal of the spiritual life including prayer and faith in Christ, a reappropriation of the founding charism, and responsiveness to the signs of the times. These transforming qualities will not be found in outward, organisational change but in our inward experience of living the Quaker Way.

Here I believe we come to the crux of the challenges facing us. When modern Friends hear the collective experience of the Quaker tradition, some of us find it expressed in language that does not to match our own experiences. Trinitarian or biblical expressions or spoken prayer can alienate some Friends, gender inclusive language for God can distress others, and gender exclusive language can offend many more. Exploration of an appropriate language to convey religious experience is beyond the scope of this lecture. However, it is an essential task to be faced by Friends in the long term if we are to find a corporate identity beyond our collective disparities.

In the meantime we cannot wait until it becomes easy to share our experience and to find where God's story is woven into our story. The diversity we so highly value will become a meaningless jumble if we cannot communicate our own parts of the pattern to one another.

To communicate we need to express our own experience and to listen to that of others. The Chinese characters that make up the verb 'to listen' tell us something about what listening will require of us. The characters are: 'ear', 'you', 'eyes', 'undivided attention', 'heart'. The kind of listening we need to do, one with another, is to attend to 'where words come from'.[66]

Renewal of the spiritual life

The first part of this lecture pointed out that many in our meetings hunger for a renewed spiritual life. This hunger has prompted some Friends to search extensively for meaning among a variety of religious or psychoanalytic experiences; it has less often prompted a deep search of the Quaker tradition itself. This is understandable. For those who fled from oppression, rigidity and exclusion in other churches to the more open atmosphere of Quakerism, it can be surprising and difficult to discover that much of the Quaker tradition has used language and imagery we thought we were leaving behind.

Hidden riches in the Quaker tradition may be obscured by religious jargon or by our own preconceptions. Only by looking beyond difficult words or images can we find, in the writings of early Friends, our own experience of living by the inward guide. Looking back at the tradition is not a matter of studying ideas. Following George Fox's practice, we can read from scripture or the writings of early Friends not primarily to understand them intellectually, but to participate in the experiences that inspired the words: experiences that satisfy the mind and the heart and go beyond them both.

From the Puritan and Christ-centred roots of early Quakerism has grown a spirituality that can empower and free us today. Greater familiarity with the long story of the tradition will free us, not bind us: we can see better where we may be led in future by understanding where and how we have been led in the past. We will have an accurate assessment of the tradition, not settling for flattering fantasies about 'The Quakers', nor being deluded that we are other than the fallible, wrongheaded yet graced people that we are. Most of all, secure in our own tradition, we will be able to draw freely on the religious experiences of others. Marjorie Sykes, a British Friend who lived most of her life in India, said:

> 'What think ye of Christ?' is central both in our relationships with other religions and in our relationship with one another within the Society of Friends... We are truly loyal to Jesus Christ when we judge the religious systems of the world by the standards which he himself used: 'Not every one that saith unto me Lord, Lord... but he that doeth the will of my Father'. Every tree is to be known by its fruits: not its dead wood, or thorns, or parasites, but by the fruit of its own inner life and nature. We all know the fruits of the Spirit, and recognise the beauty of holiness, in our ancestral tree... The flowers of unselfish living may be found growing in other men's gardens and... rich fruits of the Spirit may be tasted from other men's trees. They spring from the same Holy

Spirit of Truth, the same Seed of God, whose power moves us
through Christ.[67]

Those who have followed a spiritual path for many years will
recognise the spiritual cycle described in many earlier Friends'
writings: when we feel growing dissatisfaction with our present
spiritual state, we become willing to take risks, to respond to the
inward guide; as we take the risks under guidance, we grow, creating
more room for the Spirit to move through the cracks of our old
defences. Spiritual growth is thus a cumulative process for each
individual, and this is also true for the community. Dissatisfaction
with the spiritual state of the Religious Society of Friends can be seen
as a sign of growth, not an occasion for despair.

Renewal of the Society waits for the choice of each Friend: Am I
willing to risk the disturbing, transfiguring presence of the Spirit in
my life? To obey it? To expect 'the Cross' and dark days as I discover
and nurture who I am before God? When we choose to live the spiritual life the Quaker Way, these are the experiences we are committing
ourselves to, whatever words we put upon them. If significant
numbers of us are not interested in, or willing to live by these
experiences, the hoped-for renewal of our meetings cannot occur. But
if our collective spiritual power gathers strength it will infect other
Friends and newcomers. Ministry will become more grounded in the
Spirit and individuals will be inspired by the Spirit to serve our
meetings as nurturers, prophets and conservers.

Reappropriation of the founding charism

Although we need to see clearly who early Friends were, we should
not try to copy them. George Fox taught us a spiritual process that will
lead us to Truth for our own time. We are to live out in our own time
the unique Quaker Way or talent that God has entrusted to us through
generations of faithful Friends. Friends have a particular holy gift for
our own lives and for our world. In its theological guise we call this
gift 'realised eschatology', living now in the Kingdom or the Reign of
God; or, more simply, 'living in the solution'. None of these terms
adequately conveys the challenge of being asked to live in the present

as if God's view of the world were realistic or even possible.

In the topsy-turvey world of the Way of God as taught by Jesus, familiar categories turn upside down: people with contagious diseases are touched and healed; a woman who prefers intellectual discussions to housework is highly valued; the unemployed get a day's wage for a few hours' work; a prostitute is held up as a good example to a religious leader; the good seats at a state banquet go to the street people; and a woman with a just cause gets what she wants – because she nags.

The Quaker tradition testifies that by the insight and power of the inward guide it is possible for us to live comfortably today in the upside-down world of the Way of God, the reign that is both here and now and not yet.

I have come to appreciate the uniqueness of this Quaker perspective partly through living with my familiars: fruit bats. *Pteropus,* large fruit bats with prominent eyes, soft black fur and a wingspan of over five feet despite their small bodies, are widely considered by scientists to be a type of primate: humans' nearest relatives in Australia. I have been involved for several years in hand-raising orphaned fruit bats to be released in the wild, through the Organisation for Native Animals Rescue and Release (ONARR) in southeast Queensland. My observations at the bat–human interface have always been a source of reflection and prayer, but in recent years fruit bats have become a symbol of the grace and flexibility required of me to live the Way of God.

Bats can look at the world upside down, or rightside up, depending on whether they are hanging or flying. Living with them one gets used to their capacity to live topsy-turvey, in two dimensions at once. Humans are less adaptable: to look at a bat, even in a photograph, most people automatically turn the bat's head upward so as to see her 'rightside up'. Human babies delight in seeing the world upside down, but this joyful flexibility rarely persists in our adult lives. The bat's talent of finding herself rightside up in an upside-down world can be ours too: the vision and power of the inward guide bestows on us the flexibility and wisdom to live God's Way – now!

The charism of early Friends was their gift of sight and action to live at home in the upside-down world of God's reign. We need to reclaim their gift of seeing the Way of God clearly despite the disturbance and distraction of their times. We need to find in ourselves their gift of publicly testifying as a community to the Way of God. Plainness of speech, behaviour and dress were outward signs that early Friends used as a way of pointing to God's values in seventeenth-century England. What signs can we construct today?

Responsiveness to the signs of our times

Over the course of their history, Friends have responded in a variety of ways to the world around them. In the eighteenth century, Friends testified to God's values by living them strictly, apart from the world. Early Friends and nineteenth-century evangelical Friends felt responsible for the spiritual, and sometimes the material, wellbeing of those around them and took God's values into the marketplace. Whether Friends interpreted their tradition as requiring them to be involved in the world, or to be apart from it, they have always expected that their Quaker values would diverge markedly from the norms of the wider society in which they found themselves.

Learning to respond to the signs of our times, modern Friends have a double resource in the Quaker tradition of inward waiting and active persistence. This tradition calls for giving careful attention to the inward guide, in the inspiration of the individual and in the discernment of the community, and then matching this inward focus with the hard experience of living out testimonies that are not at home in the world. The lessons of inward waiting and outward persistence in the Quaker Way are as applicable within our meetings as they are to the wider social challenges outside our communities.

Australian Friends have been seeking to strengthen our meetings, looking for better ways to be a community: to provide eldership and oversight, to include attenders (and members) in the life of the Meeting, and to make nominations and appointments. We are discussing the purpose of membership itself. Self-scrutiny in our corporate life matches the pattern of personal spiritual exploration traced at the beginning of this lecture. These signs of dissatisfaction and searching prepare us for growth. We grow personally and together by responding to the guidance we find within, led and empowered by the Spirit.

> Return home to within, sweep your houses all, the groat is there, the little leaven is there, the grain of mustard-seed you will see, which the Kingdom of God is like; ...and here you will see your Teacher not removed into a corner, but present when you are upon your beds and about your labour, convincing, instructing, leading, correcting, judging and giving peace to all that love and follow Him.[68]

Conclusion

I write the last words of this lecture from Woodbrooke in England, as autumn leaves begin to drift past my window. Coming to the end, it has been tempting to put forward my own views about the Way forward for Australian Quakers at the end of the twentieth century: words about our business methods, testimonies, changes in eldership and oversight, committees for clearness, and our life of worship and prayer and concerns. In the phrase of eighteenth-century Friends, to do so would have 'outstripped my guide'.

It would also have cut across the movement of this lecture which has asked Friends to focus on the *how* of the Quaker Way, exploring from the perspectives of the past, the limitations and the possibilities of our future. In the Quaker Way the transcendent and immanent aspects of our lives are indivisible; the spiritual vitality of our meetings depends on each of us being faithful to the inward guide; and action for justice to transform the world arises from our inward awareness of God's way in the world.

There are new challenges and changes sweeping British Quakerism and Australian Quakerism as we struggle to give birth to renewed communities, but the specific structures are less important than how we formulate them and how we use them. They will be Life-giving if they reflect our fidelity to divine guidance and are lived flexibly yet tenaciously under that same guidance.

Living upside down in the rightside-up world, we are asked to be and to do many things seemingly beyond human wisdom or power.

Colonies of fruit bats unexpectedly (at least by human wisdom) fly hundreds of kilometres to a forest of native blossom that has not flowered for years. There they feed on nectar and pollinate the hardwoods. If we are open to the Spirit, the signs of our times and our Quaker heritage, we will find new and unexpected places to give the fertility needed by the world, taking our own nourishment at the same time.

NOTES

This book was first published in 1993, before the change from 'London' to 'Britain' Yearly Meeting, and the publication of *Quaker faith & practice* in 1995 (cited as *QF&P*).

1   Rowntree, J.W., in *Christian faith and practice,* London Yearly Meeting 1972 (cited hereafter as *CF&P*), §94 (1905) [not in *QF&P*].
2   Macmurray, J., *Search for reality in religion,* London: Friends Home Service Committee 1965, p.34.
3   Dann, G.M.S., 'Religious belonging in a changing Catholic church', *Sociological Analysis* 1976, 37:287.
4   Palmer, P., *To know as we are known,* San Francisco: Harper & Row 1983, p.14.
5   Rahner, K., *A Rahner reader,* ed. G.A. McCool, London: Darton, Longman & Todd 1975, pp.20-21, 30, 45.
6   Ruether, R.R., *Sexism and God-talk,* London: SCM Press 1983.
7   Haughton, R., *The passionate God,* London: Darton, Longman & Todd 1981.
8   Biser, E., 'Limitations of religious communication', *Communicatio-Socialis* 1980, 13:299-320.
9   Needleman, J., *A sense of the cosmos,* New York: Dutton 1976, p.170.
10 Braithwaite, W.C., *Spiritual guidance in the experience of the Society of Friends,* London: Headley Brothers 1909.
11 Reynolds, R., *The wisdom of John Woolman,* London: FHSC 1972.
12 Fitz, R. & L. Cada, 'The recovery of religious life', *Review for Religious* 1975, 34:679-707.
13 Punshon, J., *Portrait in grey,* London: Quaker Home Service 1984.
14 Isichei, E.A., *Victorian Quakers,* London: Oxford U.P. 1970, p.66.
15 Hill, C., *The world turned upside down,* London: Temple Smith 1972.
16 Bacon, M.H., *Mothers of feminism,* San Francisco: Harper & Row 1986, p.6.
17 Fox, G., in *CF&P,* §9 (1647) [*QF&P,* §26.03].
18 Underhill, E., *Mysticism,* New York: Dutton 1961, p.469.
19 Fox, G., *The journal of George Fox,* ed. J.L. Nickalls, London Yearly Meeting 1975, p.143 (1652).
20 Fox, in *CF&P,* §10 (1648) [*QF&P,* §28.03].

21 Fox, *Journal, op.cit.,* p.27 (1648).

22 Fox, G., Epistle 172, 1659, in *'The power of the Lord is over all',* ed. T.C. Jones, Richmond, Indiana: Friends United Press 1989, p.132.

23 Edward Burrough, quoted in W.C. Braithwaite, *The beginnings of Quakerism,* London: Macmillan 1970, p.320.

24 Fox, Epistle 37, 1653, in Jones, ed., *op.cit.,* p.132.

25 Fox, in *CF&P,* §406 (1652) [*QF&P,* §20.42].

26 Sewel, W., 1722, in E.F. Norlind, *The atonement of George Fox,* ed. E.P. Mather, Philadelphia: Pendle Hill Pamphlet 166, 1969, p.5.

27 Barbour, H., *The Quakers in puritan England,* Richmond, Indiana: Friends United Press 1985, p.31.

28 Gwyn, D., *Apocalypse of the Word: the life and message of George Fox (1624 -1691),* Richmond, Indiana: Friends United Press 1986, p.20.

29 Holden, D., *Friends divided,* Richmond, Indiana: Friends United Press 1988, p.7.

30 Gwyn, *op.cit.,* p.20.

31 Vipont, E., *George Fox and the valiant sixty,* London: Hamish Hamilton 1975.

32 Bacon, *op.cit,* p.19.

33 Hill, *op.cit.*

34 Bacon, *op.cit,* p.19.

35 Bauman, R., *Let your words be few,* Cambridge U.P. 1983, p.27.

36 Ellwood, T., in *CF&P,* §36 (1659) [*QF&P,* §19.16].

37 Barclay, R., in *CF&P,* §41 (1676) [*QF&P,* §19.21].

38 Fox, Epistle 313, 1674, in Jones, ed., *op.cit.,* p.312.

39 Willauer, G.J., 'First publishers of truth in New England: a composite list 1656-1775', *Quaker History* Spring 1976, 65:35-44.

40 Braithwaite, 1970, *op.cit.,* pp.140-141.

41 Barbour, *op.cit.,* p.118.

42 Bittle, W., *James Nayler 1618 -1660,* York: Sessions 1986, p.108.

43 Bittle, *op.cit.,* p.95.

44 Writing from Launceston prison: 'James! Thou must beare thy owne Burden, & thy Companyes with thee whose Iniquity doth increase & by thee is not cried against...' This letter from GF was found on JN at his arrest in Bristol and helped to exonerate the Quaker movement as a whole from JN's action.

45 Fox, *Journal, op.cit.,* p.269 (1656).

46 Punshon, *op.cit.,* p.75; for more on this complex struggle see Bittle, *op.cit.,* p.99.

47 Barbour, *op.cit.,* pp.66-67; Punshon, *op.cit.,* pp.76-77; Sheeran, M., *Beyond majority rule,* Philadelphia Yearly Meeting 1983, pp.12-14.

48 Braithwaite, 1970, *op.cit.,* p.271.

49 Fox, *Journal, op.cit.,* pp.281-284.

50 Braithwaite, W.C., *The second period of Quakerism,* London: Macmillan 1919, p.115.

51 Fox, Epistle 162, 1658, in Jones, ed., *op.cit.,* p.124 [*QF&P,* §3.30].

52 Braithwaite, 1919, *op.cit.,* p.276.

53 Braithwaite, *ibid.,* pp.282, 297-298.

54 Sheeran, *op.cit.,* pp.29-38.

55 Braithwaite, 1919, *op.cit.,* p.516.

56 Sheeran, *op.cit.,* p.41.

57 Bownas, S., in *CF&P,* §45 (1696) [*QF&P,* §19.60].

58 Damiano, K., *On earth as it is in heaven: eighteenth-century Quakerism as realised eschatology,* Cincinnati, Ohio: UMI Dissertation Services, p.45; this work gives a clear view of the vitality of 'quietist' Quakerism.

59 Fox, Epistle 264, 1669, in Jones, *op.cit.,* p.256.

60 Jones, R., in D. Steere, ed., *Quaker spirituality: selected writings,* London: SPCK 1984, pp.267, 270.

61 Rowntree, J.W., quoted in introduction to §94, *CF&P* [not in *QF&P*].

62 Isichei, *op.cit.,* pp.40-67.

63 Barclay, R., *Apology for the true Christian divinity,* publ. in London in Latin (1676) and English (1678).

64 Brown, T., 'Equipping for ministry', preliminary paper for Equipping for Ministry Conference, London Yearly Meeting, 24-27 August 1990, p.3.

65 Oats, W., *A question of survival: Quakers in Australia in the nineteenth century,* Brisbane: Queensland University Press 1985, pp.78-126.

66 Papunahung, a chief of Indians at Wyalusing in Pennsylvania, did not require a translator when listening to John Woolman, and said, 'I love to hear where words come from'. Reynolds, *op.cit.,* p.28.

67 Sykes, M., in *CF&P,* §226 (1957) [*QF&P,* §27.11].

68 Howgill, F., in *CF&P,* §176 (1656) [*QF&P,* §26.71].